Huronia Apr/82 25-

The last move was made in 1963

Mrs. Hood sold the business in 1954 to Mr. Wallace. Other owners since then have been the redoubtable Julia Jarvis, Jean Tweed and Lawrence Cooper. In 1963, the Book Room moved to its present site on Ross Street and it was there that I went a few days ago to talk about the store and see what I could find on the shelves.

For my weird tastes, there were some terrific buys: a collection of speeches by George Brown, founder of this newspaper; a turn-of-the-century account of the Methodist missionary service in China; an unintentionally funny novel by Sir Francis Bond Head (the early governor of Upper Canada who makes the hit-list of all constitutionally progressive historians); and a copy of Kathleen Coburn's The Grandmothers, a wonderfully insightful and warm account of two intrepid ladies who lit up their small worlds with such enthusiasm for life and adept manipulation of harsh realities that you wonder why we were never wise enough to let them rule the world.

The store's business history is curious. It was one of the main sources of new Canadian publications for libraries all over the world and it was this trade which kept things bubbling at Dora Hood's for decades.

Courtesy "The Globe and Mail"

DORA HOOD AND HER DAUGHTER, GLEN

THE SIDE DOOR

Twenty-six Years in My Book Room

Dora Hood

THE RYERSON PRESS ~ TORONTO

Published 1958

PRINTED AND BOUND IN CANADA
BY THE RYERSON PRESS, TORONTO

To the memory of my husband
Frederick Colton Hood, M.D.

PREFACE

THE SUGGESTION THAT I SHOULD write an account of my life in my Book Room was made to me by Dr. W. Stewart Wallace and Dr. Lorne Pierce, men whose judgment otherwise I respect. From 1928 to 1954 they had been aware of growth of the business, but they had no means of knowing whether my ability to write a second-hand book catalogue implied authorship in a much more sustained effort. Lapses on this score must not be laid at their door. I am grateful to these two friends for their encouragement. The task has given me many hours of keen pleasure and not a few, I confess, of inadequacy.

I have been fortunate, too, in possessing another helpful friend. Miss Julia Jarvis volunteered to read the manuscript and by her discriminating suggestions the text has been vastly improved.

A book about buying and selling books might be expected to quote prices. But prices, like clothes, go out of date and as the years pass may appear ridiculous.

I am constrained to add a word of thanks to my two children, Wharton and Glen. I could not have accomplished what I did had they not been the best children a mother ever had.

DORA HOOD.

CONTENTS

1. Beginner's Luck

And what is one's life without chances?
Ye've always a chance with the tide.
Jean Barlow.

It was by chance rather than by design that I became a bookseller.

It came about in this way. I dined one evening with my friend, Jeanette Rathbun, and the conversation turned to the congenial subject of books. I was surprised to hear her say rather wearily that she was tired of books. She then confessed that for more than two years she had been attempting to carry on a mail-order book business in her spare time, which meant the evenings, for she had a full daytime occupation. She had at one time hoped she might make the books her business, but now she knew she could not drop her salaried work in favour of the uncertainty of selling books.

After dinner I asked to see the books and found that they were all out-of-print books on Canada. I think this was the first time I had encountered the euphonious word "Canadiana" as applied to books and it was most emphatically the first time I had seen such a minute and tidy second-hand bookshop; for such it was. She had issued a few catalogues and had compiled a small mailing list and her files and account books were models of neatness. I began to ask questions. Where did she get her stock of books? That was the difficulty, she confessed. In her limited time she could not look for them and keeping strictly to mail-order it was difficult to expand. It had almost ceased to be a paying enterprise. I stayed late but finally tore myself away and stepped out into the windy March night. I liked what I had seen of that small book business. It had a powerful appeal to me and I thought of nothing else all the way home. Suddenly, as I neared my house I found myself saying out loud to the swaying elm trees: "That is what I want to do! I'll make her an offer." By the time I had turned the key in my door, I had taken the first steps on a journey which was not to end for twenty-six years.

In a short time satisfactory arrangements had been completed and I was in possession of a business about which I knew nothing. Looking back over this period, I do not remember having had the slightest misgivings about my ability to become a bookseller, although up to this time no experience in my life had included money making. But things were different now. I had six months before become a widow and I knew I must add to my small income in order to keep myself and my two small children. If all went well, this was the answer.

I had two assets. On the intangible side, I knew I had a certain awareness of books. On the tangible, a house that would lend itself to such an enterprise. It had four good-sized rooms, one behind the other, on the ground floor and it was on a street which was fast turning from a residential to a business one. I felt it might be possible, with the help of a housekeeper, to bring up my family and at the same time conduct a business. I think on the whole I found the latter job the less difficult.

I remember vividly the first few weeks of my business career. Nothing could have been more unbusinesslike.

I pushed the furniture to the back of my long old-fashioned drawing room and moved in a large utilitarian steel bookcase, a typewriter, and a massive steel letter file; and then the books arrived. As I unpacked them and spread them out on the Persian rug, I thought I had never seen a more uninteresting collection in my life. But I was wrong and, as time went on, I learned not to judge books by their outward appearance. This was the nucleus around which was to gather, and disperse, as the years passed, many thousands of Canadian books and pamphlets.

I had no intention of keeping my trade to mail order only and hopefully expected a steady stream of customers once it became known that such a shop existed. Little did I know that collectors of Canadiana were few and widely scattered across our great country and that most men's thoughts were otherwise engaged in 1928—that year of wild speculation and easy money.

Nevertheless, a few letters began to arrive via the old address and it was necessary to decide on a distinctive name. As books are a commodity of individual taste, I reasoned perhaps the buyers would like to know that they were dealing with a person rather than with a company, and since men use their own names in business, why should I not use mine? The prefix "Mrs." sounded old-fashioned, even Victorian, so I decided to leave it out and as, in its present form, the business could hardly be called a shop, it became and remained Dora Hood's Book Room. I do not think any other name was considered. The public, uncertain as to how to address such an establishment, in general solved the problem by the usual "Dear Sir." But curiosity got the better of some of them. A customer in Quebec begged to be forgiven, but he felt he must know whether the lady he was addressing was a Mrs. or a Miss. Later we became great friends but I failed to find out whether I would have been more acceptable as a single woman. Was I handicapped by being a woman proprietor of a second-hand bookshop? I do not think this occurred to me in the busy early years of my enterprise. But later, when I was well established, I knew I had to prove myself in a field where men almost exclusively had held sway.

I had scarcely arranged my small stock in alphabetical order on the steel bookshelves when I was confronted with the problem which was to test my judgment and school me in the art of making quick decisions. This was what I afterwards grew to know as a "deal." Fortunately, I had a delightful person to deal with in Mr. Jull, who for many years after remained a friend. He must have been one of the very first of the long line of collectors who found their way to the Book Room. Perhaps it was to give a welcome to the newcomer in the antiquarian book business as well as a true love of Canadian books that led Mr. Jull to inspect my shelves.

Among my original stock was a complete set of *The Review of Historical Publications Relating to Canada.* edited by George M. Wrong and Hugh Langton. There were twenty-four volumes and they covered the years 1897-1920. They are severe looking books bound in a muddy brown cloth. In after years I learned to respect this set for it was the first sustained attempt to estimate the value of historical works in Canada as they appeared. It is still consulted as a bibliography with the added value of criticism and appreciation, and from it developed the present *Canadian Historical Review.*

When Mr. Jull had examined all my books he asked if I would consider allowing him to have the *Review* in exchange for some of the books from his library which he no longer needed. It was not difficult to be agreeable where Mr. Jull was concerned, and that evening he and his son returned with several cartons of books. At least, I thought, these books all had different titles and such names, though new to me, as *Our Forest Home* and *In the Days of the Canada Company,* sounded attractive. I decided to take the risk and the deal was closed. Mr. Jull appeared happy as he carried away his dull brown set and I sat down on the floor to inspect my new possessions.

My first mail order did not have such a happy ending, however. After all the intervening years it is strange how every detail of this episode remains in my memory. The order came from a man in Montreal for *Index and Dictionary of Canadian History* issued with the first series of the set known as *Makers of Canada.* I searched my meagre supply of books; there it was, conveniently marked $3. I was delighted to type my first invoice, carefully wrap, weigh and dispatch the parcel. It was somewhat disconcerting to have the book returned a week later with a note to say he had decided the book was not worth the price. I stood firm and did not reduce it, for by that time other orders had come in. I had my foot on the first rung of the ladder and was not dismayed.

What preparation had I for embarking on such an enterprise? None, or so it seemed at the time. I was in my early forties and my school days seemed far away and my education had not included a university degree. Most girls of my Edwardian upbringing neither went to university nor took office jobs, both of which might have been to my advantage. But, though Canadian born, I had spent the middle of my school years in England and because history, there, was on our door steps, I had taken a special course in it at the Perce School for Girls in Cambridge. I remember my pretty and learned history mistress presenting me with a book called *Source Book of English History,* and asking me to tell her what it meant.

I hadn't the least idea! Twenty-five years later I was to make a living out of buying and selling source books of Canadian history in the form of Government documents, annual reports, narratives of explorers, letters, diaries and innumerable other first-hand accounts of the unfolding of our country's history. I do not remember ever having studied Canadian history even during my years in a Canadian school, yet I did gain through my later reading and through family traditions a vague outline of the short but stirring annals of our country. And so it seems that even an education as pleasant and irregular as mine may some day be turned to good account.

My first catalogue was issued in February, 1929. There were four hundred and eighty-one book titles and thirty-eight pamphlets in it and in bold letters on the front page it announced, "MANY INTERESTING ITEMS RECENTLY PURCHASED—NOTE THE PRICES!" After twenty-eight years it is well worth while to note the prices, for like everything else many books have gone up in value, due to the old law of supply and demand. But not all of them, I hasten to add, for fashions change in books as in other commodities. I notice one which lapsed in popularity and now will probably be in demand again.

In 1886 the publishers of a weekly called *Grip* put out two volumes called *A Caricature History of Canadian Politics*. These were drawn by J. W. Bengough and underneath were biting comments by the same hand. There had been an earlier series of two smaller volumes bound in one in 1875 so that it may be seen that the politicians had for a long time to put up with a good deal of fun at their expense. These books had always sold well since there were still living many who remembered the stalwarts here depicted in various unflattering situations. Then the jokes and pictures lost their appeal for a time, to be revived as illustrations for Donald Creighton's stirring life of Sir John A. Macdonald, where they supplement the familiar photographs with a spicy touch of the times in keeping with the text.

In 1939 an old gentleman walked into my office and asked if I had any copies of *Grip*. I had a bundle of them but, as I told him, it was next to impossible to collate a whole set since they had been issued so irregularly. "I know," he said, "for I am the last surviving brother of the five Bengoughs, and I am over ninety." He said he was anxious to collect four complete sets for his children and now needed only a few numbers. He then sat down and wrote me a memo of the important dates in the history of the publishing firm. I give it now, as I do not think it appears elsewhere in print. I never saw my old informant again.

GRIP (Weekly Paper)
J. W. Bengough, ed. and artist.
T. Bengough, printer.

May 24, 1873, to Dec. 29, 1894.

1875 G. Bengough came in.
Called Bengough Bros.

1881 J. W. Bengough, S. J. Moore & G. Bengough.

1883 Grip Printing Publishing Co.
Ran paper until July, 1893.
Then suspended at Ser. No. 1048.

1894 Jan. 4 – 1st No. of N.S. (whole 1049).
Phoenix Publishing Co. (J. W. Bengough, J. J. Bell)
81 Adelaide St. West.
Ran until 1894. Dec.

While most of the books in my first catalogue were out of print I ventured to list a few new books which seemed to fit into it. One of them got me into a good deal of trouble and taught me a lesson, though eventually I reaped a rich reward. This book is called *Peter Pond, Fur*

Trader and Adventurer, by H. A. Innis. (Toronto, Irwin and Gordon, 1930). The publishers were two young men who had had little experience in the difficult task of launching a book in Canada. They came to me, rather to my surprise, to help them. Would I list it in my catalogue, they asked? I was assured it would be ready in plenty of time and they gave me some advance advertising, so that I could write an attractive description. This gave me the idea of listing several others, which appeared on the inside front cover. The day came when the 1,500 copies of the catalogue were rolled up and addressed and submitted to the not always tender care of the post office. Almost overnight orders from it began to arrive in a flood. This was success beyond my dreams, and almost every order included *Peter Pond*. He was a best seller. Everyone wanted to know more about his weary journeys across our endless Northwest. I rang up the publishers and announced with pride the good news, only to be told that the map, Pond's own, the first of the West, was not yet printed and it would be some time before it could be expected. There was no way out of it for me. Apology, explanation, and often money returned was the order of the days that followed. It was then that I started my first "Books Wanted" file, and *Peter Pond* cards outnumbered all the others. It was more than a year before the map was ready and I was able to announce the book was now complete. Soon afterwards the unfortunate publishers closed their doors and the stock was taken over by The Ryerson Press. From then on *Peter Pond* was never absent from my "Fur Traders" shelf. It remained one of my steady sellers until I retired and the book was finally pronounced "out of print."

One of my first big orders came from Rhodes House Library in Oxford. It consisted of sheet after sheet of titles and I was given *carte blanche* to supply them as soon as possible. This almost proved my undoing but as so often happened in my career I was saved by the help of a bibliophile at the critical moment. The order asked for a great variety of Parliamentary Papers, and I knew nothing about them. Somehow I must puzzle them out for myself, I thought. I could not afford to fail. It was a relief to hear the door open and to be confronted by a rather shabbily dressed middle-aged man with a large paper parcel under his arm. He asked if he could show me some books which he wanted to sell, and we were soon deep in an enlightening discussion of Canadian books. It was evident that here was a heaven-sent answer to my troubles. I told him my predicament. I could not have chosen a better guide, for Mr. H., it appeared, was a staunch Conservative, had served as a "whip" in his younger days, and had a voice grown husky from many a speech on the hustings extolling the virtues of his own party and the vile behaviour of the opposition. He came many times and with infinite patience unravelled the tangled threads that make up the pattern of Government documents. Debates and Journals in the Senate and Commons, Sessional papers and Archives and the mysterious publications known as "returns" and "appendices" became as familiar to me, as the years rolled on, as my daily newspaper. Of course, I bought Mr. H.'s books as little by little he parted with his collection. They were not valuable in the market but they were priceless to me. He saved the day for one ignorant young bookseller and he deserved an end less fraught with financial worries.

Many years later I had to supply the new Government of India with all the publications on the vital subject of Confederation. This I was able to do and they all went out by air in the diplomatic bag. I sometimes wondered who studied these heavy tomes and whether my contribution had influenced the turn of world events.

The Book Room was a new experience in the lives of my two children, aged seven and ten. It needed a rapid change in my behaviour sometimes to turn from the ingratiating bookseller to the stern parent when occasion arose. Once I arrived in the office to find my seven-year-old daughter already there and in the act of displaying an illustrated book to an amused customer, with the remark, "Now this is a very nice book!" Fifteen years later she became my chief cataloguer and we worked together until the time of her marriage. It was a family occasion for us to sit around the dining-room table and to roll and tie up the catalogues ready for posting, until increasing homework put an end to my children's part in it.

It was six months before I realized I had a full-time occupation on my hands. Gradually my hours at work lengthened and often I worked far into the night, when the house was quiet, with my cat for company curled up on one of the wire baskets on my desk.

There was no time to learn to type properly and I soon became aware that my letters needed more expert handling than I could give them. As the depression increased there was no difficulty in getting expert stenographers. It was a distressing sight to see crowds of these well-trained and capable girls putting in their enforced leisure at the Y.W.C.A. It was there that I engaged Elma and her gratitude was out of all proportion to the salary I could offer her. She stayed with me for several years and developed a real flair for selling and a workable knowledge of the stock.

With the laborious work of trying to type removed, I was able to develop another side of the business which was thrust upon me. Librarians in the United States who had ordered from my catalogues began to send orders for current publications. While sometimes we had to hunt for some obscure book or periodical, on the whole it was work I could leave to my assistant if necessary, and the profits, if small, were sure. It built up, as time passed, interesting contacts with some of the great university libraries.

The University of California at Berkeley used this agency service throughout the whole of my business life. It was not until 1951, however, that the opportunity came unexpectedly to visit the library. I was in Victoria, B.C., when a friend asked me if I would fly with her to San Francisco. Her main idea in taking the trip was to replenish her supply of shoes, while I was charmed to have a chance to see the legendary city and to pay a call on my clients at Berkeley.

I wrote to the head of the order department to say that I was coming and on arrival found a nice note of welcome and a pressing invitation to come any day convenient to me.

The town of Berkeley, which is reached from San Francisco by an eight-mile bridge, is a place of little distinction. But the University is set on the slopes leading to the high hills which surround the famous harbour of San Francisco, and the campus itself is beautiful.

I took my travelling companion along to the interview, for in truth I felt very small and unimportant when I considered that this University was said to have the largest student body of any university in the world. We were ushered into the imposing office of the head of the order department and to my astonishment the place was filled with important-looking persons who turned out to be the heads of all the other departments in this enormous library. I was rather overcome by this reception although, when introduced to them, most of their names were household words in our office. I hope I carried off the ordeal with sufficient aplomb, for I could see by a side glance at my friend that she was impressed by the reception given to an obscure Canadian bookseller. The atmosphere became friendly as we discussed problems connected with our work together and in due course we were put into the care of a delightful woman, to be shown over the building. The luxurious reading rooms—more conducive to sleep than study, I thought—the modern cafeterias, the special collections of rare books, all bespoke unlimited funds upon which the authorities could draw. The students who thronged the halls and recreation rooms were a cross-section of the nations of the world. One looked in vain for a typical American face. Orientals may not have been in the majority but they were conspicuously numerous. It was obvious that the students were there for work and not for play.

When I returned to the Book Room the familiar California orders thereafter called up a mental picture of that surging crowd of seekers after the printed word.

The time came more quickly than I had anticipated when more space was essential in the Book Room. The family retreated to a smaller room and the erstwhile drawing-room became wholly an office. More bookcases were fitted in, the fireplace was taken away, and the table on which we wrapped our parcels was moved to the hall. Still the room could hardly have been called businesslike. There remained chintz curtains, the Chippendale bookcase and the Persian rug. I had qualms about the wear on the latter until assured by the rug man who cleaned it that that kind of rug was intended for use in mosques and would wear a hundred years.

While my business had widened to include Canadian books still in print I determined that my main objective would be the supplying of out-of-print and rare Canadian works. It would always be my aim to take as much pleasure in locating an obscure and inexpensive book or pamphlet as in supplying, say, a Jesuit *Relation*.

By 1936, in spite of the depression, the Book Room had developed "growing pains." The room and hall that seemed so spacious at first had grown uncomfortably crowded and each new purchase added to our problems. My children, too, were demanding more space for themselves and their friends as they grew into adolescence.

There were still two large rooms on the ground floor, an old-fashioned ample kitchen, and next to it an unnecessarily large dining-room. I decided on drastic measures to deal with a desperate need. I would make these two back rooms into offices and leave the front two for our living quarters with amidships, so to speak, a small modern kitchen.

My architect, the late Herbert Horner, proved a man of deep understanding. He said it could be done by the simple means of taking down one wall here and putting another up there, by turning a window into a door and thereby giving my customers direct access to the books. This returned the front door to exclusive use by the family and avoided inevitable collisions with important clients.

But it wasn't quite as simple as that. To alter a house and still live in it, to say nothing of conducting a business at the same time, proved too much for me. I stood it for a few weeks, then covering up the books as best I could, I fled to Muskoka and tried not to think of what was happening at home.

When I returned, despite dust and general confusion, I knew I had made the right decision. It only remained to move the bookcases and then the books into the rear offices, no small task.

The bookcases fitted into the new wall space as though they had been measured for it, which they were not. I had merely trusted to luck and the results were better than I deserved. All hands were needed to transfer the books. Dust flew, chaos reigned, books mysteriously lost turned up and in the midst of it all the household cat was vainly looking for her favourite wire basket.

With the posting of the "Book Room" sign on the side door a new era had begun.

2. Early Adventures in Book Buying

The monument of vanished minds.
— Davenant.

My introduction to the business of selling second-hand books was coincident with the development of the depression of the nineteen-thirties. This might have been disastrous to an enterprise such as mine with no reserve capital, but by a quirk of circumstances I actually benefited by the recession as my early adventures in book buying proved.

Part of the charm of keeping a second-hand book shop, I soon learned, is the uncertainty of where your next supply of books is coming from. I do not remember having worried about this, even in the early days of my venture. Very few weeks passed when no books were offered to me. To be sure, they were not always the ones I most needed, but that too added to the spice of life. It was comparatively simple to buy a dozen or so books, but quite another proposition to be offered a large library when one was as inexperienced as I was. I was fortunate, I know now, in being offered good libraries for at that time I had few competitors who were willing to put their capital into books.

One of my earliest experiences in book buying led me to a strange house and resulted in a profitable find.

My friend, Mr. Paul Hahn, an ardent stamp collector, had developed an uncanny knack of discovering places where stamps of value would likely be found. One day he asked me to go with him to a house on the corner of Sherbourne and Howard Streets where he hoped to get some good stamps. "It's a queer place," he said, "but it is full of books and it is possible we might induce the owner to let you have a look at them." When we reached the house I remembered it had always appeared shut up and uninhabited. The dust of years was on the unopened wooden shutters and although it was a substantial, even rather an imposing house, it had a most uninviting appearance. Our ring was answered by a very old lady, completely swathed in woollen shawls. Even her head was wrapped in an ancient knitted covering In spite of her mummy-like appearance, she greeted Mr. Hahn in a friendly manner and led us through the dark hall into the semi-darkness of an old-fashioned drawing-room. While the stamps were being discussed I had a chance to examine the room. It was handsomely furnished in the style of the 1890's. There may have been stately parties there once, but I had the feeling that the chairs had stood in their present positions, unmoved, for years. It was now 1930 and the place was still dimly lit by gas jets and probably under the enormous crinkled paper shades the lamps contained oil. The stamp transaction having been concluded, with satisfaction apparently on both sides, Mr. Hahn tactfully brought the conversation round to the subject of the books. The interview, however, came to an abrupt end and we found ourselves rather unceremoniously ushered out of the door. Mr. Hahn said he was sorry we had not been successful, but not to give up hope. The old lady lived there with her son, who was almost as much of a recluse as his mother. The father, a prominent and well-educated man, had died many years before.

It was about a year later that I had an urgent call again from Mr. Hahn. "Old Mrs. J. is dead and the son is going to sell everything in the house tomorrow. You should go down early and get the books."

Both my children were in bed with colds and I was reluctant to leave them. This seemed a usual occurrence when I had something important to do away from home. This time I knew I had to put business first. It was a dark, dreary November day when I made my way without enthusiasm across the city to the dismal house, not knowing what I should encounter this time. By nine o'clock I found myself once more on the uninviting doorstep but this time I was alone and full of apprehension. I rang the bell, there was a long wait, and I had almost persuaded myself that I would give it up, when the door was opened by a man in his nightshirt. Somewhat taken aback, I told him I had come to buy the books. Without a word he led me upstairs and into the book-lined library. I went straight to work as best I could by the dim gas jets which my silent host had lighted with a long wand-like instrument, the like of which I had not seen since childhood. Rather reluctantly I confined my selection to Canadian books, for there were many others that attracted my attention. Presently I heard the arrival of other people in the hall below, but no rival for the books appeared. There was a third storey, so up I went, to find it also filled with books, piled in cupboards and unfurnished rooms. No gas jets here, but by that time the November day had brightened and I was able to see that here were neatly tied-up bundles of early periodicals, almanacs, year books and pamphlets. I had no time to inspect them closely, my idea being to get the transaction completed before anyone else came on the scene. I carried many loads to the hall below and after about three hours of work the pile had grown to quite a formidable mountain. By this time there was much activity throughout the house. Men were carrying out the handsome old furniture and loading it into carts while the owner, now more suitably clad, stood at the door collecting, it seemed, any amount the buyers put in his hand. My modest offer for the books was readily accepted; I called a carter, helped him to transfer the mountain, took a seat beside him, and drove off across the city. It was my first big purchase. I was not at all sure that I hadn't paid too much! How wrong I was! The cellar seemed the most suitable place for such a dusty collection, and there they remained for some time.

My off-duty reading consisted of catalogues of out-of-print dealers. In those days, before the cost of printing had risen to its present heights, catalogues arrived by every mail from the United States and Europe, and from these there was much to learn of editions and prices. Periodicals for the book trade, too, were full of interesting reading. Once a month there were reports of auctions and large sections devoted to advertisements of "Books Wanted." The American Art Galleries, Anderson Galleries, New York, was then the leading auction mart of rare and valuable books and their reports were scanned with profit by most dealers. It was in one of these reports that my eye was arrested by an account of the sale of Hawthorne's *The Scarlet Letter,* first edition 1850, which had sold for $1,200. The laconic note added, "First edition having on page 21, line 22, the word 'reduplicate,' afterwards changed to 'repudiate' in 2nd issue. With advertisement tipped in. Cloth, in slip case." Instantly it flashed across my mind that somewhere in that pile of dusty books in the cellar I had seen a copy of *The Scarlet Letter.* Slipping on my dressing-gown, I made my way to the lower regions. Yes, there was the neat little volume, in such perfect condition that it might have come freshly from the press and with breathless haste I turned to page 21, line 22, and there was the magic word "reduplicate."

I had a treasure, but I was very, very young in books and had no idea how to go about getting a large price for it. This was 1930—the stock market had crashed six months before and I felt certain the time had passed for expecting fabulous sales. There was quite a stir in the little book world in Toronto when I displayed my find. Most of those I consulted told me to hold on to it as the value would undoubtedly increase. It would be something for my old age, and so on. But some instinct made me doubt the wisdom of this advice. I wrote to the American Art Galleries and told them about it. They replied they would let me know when a suitable sale was planned in which to list it. There the matter stood for some months while I returned to my own less spectacular books. At last a telegram arrived, "Send Hawthorne for inclusion in next sale. A.A."

I do not now remember what was so pressing in my life at the moment, but I know I had no time to give much thought to the decision I had to make. But I was sure this was the moment, and without further consultation with my book friends I packed the little book carefully and sent it on its way. A few weeks later I was told it had sold for $500. Now this may seem a comedown from the $1,200 of two years previous, but such is the luck in sales. The records, however, show the book has never sold since at anything like that amount. If I had kept it, the value would have diminished and I would not have been able to get even $100 for it. Refreshing my mind lately on the sales of twenty-five years ago in the Book Prices Current, it is rather satisfactory to see my copy described as the "Ansen Jones Copy" in excellent condition. All other copies brought much lower prices.

While the cheque received was highly satisfactory, the

sequel was trying to a degree. The story of the sale found its way into a corner of a Toronto newspaper, and such is the news value of books, it was copied throughout the United States and Canada. For months by every mail came offers of copies of *The Scarlet Letter,* positively the "1st ed." or perhaps—and what would I give for it? I almost wished Hawthorne had never written his masterpiece.

Apart from this find which, I hasten to say, is not a daily occurrence in the book world, there were many interesting books and pamphlets from the same purchase which enhanced my catalogues. One lot I particularly remember consisted of the earliest Canadian Almanacs and Year Books. This supply lasted me for a long time.

I am deeply indebted to Mr. Hahn for his interest in my work throughout my career as a bookseller. Never a year went by when he failed to make a call on me with the request, "Can you find me something interesting that the Library at the University would like? I want to make them a present." I usually did. He has been a member of the Champlain Society since the beginning and was always well versed in the latest volume. About the time of the annual meeting he would dash into the office saying, "I am just off to the annual meeting of the Champlain Society. They want suggestions from the members for the next publication. Have you any ideas?"

Several times I told him to suggest a new translation of Gabriel Franchère's *Relation d'un Voyage à la côte du nord-ouest de l'Amérique Septentrionale dans les années 1810, '11, '12, '13 et '14.* Montréal: De l'Imprimerie de C. B. Pasteur, 1820.

Our Toronto Public Library has in its Treasure Room the manuscript of this book purchased in 1890 from the collection of Gerald E. Hart of Montreal and New York. According to the *Bibliography of Canadiana,* edited by

Staton and Tremaine, there is a note attached to this manuscript which says:

"This MS is the original in the author's handwriting of *Franchère's Narrative of a voyage to the Northwest coast of America in the years 1811-1814,* first printed in French in Montreal in 1820 from this copy; revised and considerably altered by M. Bibaud, the historian and poet, translated into English and published by Redfield in New York in 1854. This work formed the base of Washington Irving's *Astoria.* The text as shown herein is so different to the published version, it should be reprinted verbatim as Mr. Bibaud has embellished the language considerably." (Gerald Hart)

My interest in this traveller, the first to recount his travels, in midwinter, from the Pacific coast to Montreal, had been aroused by the eagerness with which the "Redfield" edition was snapped up when it appeared in my catalogues.

Franchère was born in Montreal, travelled in Canada, and finally published his narrative there. I longed to see the first edition and towards the end of my career a copy came into my hands. It was bound in old, dry calf, the paper was roughish, and a small piece had been cut from the title page. But there it was, a very rare collector's treasure. Alas, I regret to say it did not stay in Canada but found its way by registered mail to New York.

I do not know whether the suggestion of a retranslation was ever made to the Champlain Society, but it at least has given me the chance to explain my interest in the book and Mr. Hahn's eagerness towards furthering Canadian publishing of early records.

It was continually necessary to replenish my stock. As one of my wise old neighbours once said to me, "You must have something to sell." To be sure, hers was a cake shop, but I knew it applied quite as readily to mine. When books that I wanted were offered I had to be ready to buy them, and though still timid, I was beginning to enjoy the game.

The only way to put up with the average Canadian winter is to keep so busy that you can ignore the weather. I considered the winter season was my harvest-time. My mail orders were heavy for my customers had time to sit snugly at home and peruse my catalogues, and more people drew up to my door in their warm cars and spent their Saturday afternoons looking over my stock. I enjoyed these sessions and as a rule tried to have a catalogue ready by October and another in February.

It was a bitterly cold day, I remember, when a man called me on the telephone and asked me to come at once to see the valuable collection of books he wished to sell. The voice was definitely English and the address was in Lawrence Park. Trying to reconcile this combination with a collection of Canadian books, I hesitated, only to be told sharply that if I did not come someone else would be called in. No dealer can withstand that challenge, so I went.

My taxi driver and I became completely lost in the labyrinth of roads which calls itself Lawrence Park, but at last we drew up in front of the house. It looked a most unlikely place in which to find a large library. It was all windows; not the picture type, for these had not yet arrived, but the small clustered windows which leave no wall space inside.

On being admitted, I was shown into a room much overfurnished with an ornate collection of tables, lamps, stools, chairs, and ornaments. This rather puzzled me. Surely no one would enjoy living with such a heterogeneous array, I thought. When the owner appeared I was not surprised to see him clad in the inevitable rough tweed jacket, grey flannel trousers, and presumably "old school" tie. Without much ceremony I was taken down the cellar stairs. There to my astonishment I found veritable mountains of old books, neatly piled in what might be described as a succession of peaks.

I began my usual chit-chat about books and paused to inspect the first range, but was hurried on and told to confine my inspection to those he wished to show me. I was about to assert myself, but by that time I was confronted by the pile I was asked to examine, and I knew at once I gazed on a treasure trove. Here were Canadiana of the rarest kind—books, manuscripts, letters, diaries, pamphlets. Opening one or two books I found the former owner's name, "Lawrence Heyden." This gave me a clue to the date of the collection for I knew Lawrence Heyden was born about 1835 and died at the age of seventy-one in 1906. A descendant of Robert Baldwin's family, he was a well-known personality in various parts of Canada West (Ontario), and lived at the time of his death in an old square brick house at the corner of Bloor and Bedford Road. Behind a tall hedge of lilacs the old house remained a relic of bygone days well into the twentieth century and here the two Miss Heydens lived till about 1916. Now Heyden was a bibliomaniac. He acquired books, no doubt by purchase and gift and perhaps by the not unusual method of forgetting to return them when borrowed from the owners, for many revealed the names of others. He did, however, a service to posterity by hoarding these records which possibly in other hands would have been discarded.

I knew I had to acquire these books and records no matter what they cost. Gradually I was able to convince the seller that I knew something about the history of the original owner and to induce him to tell me how he came into the possession of the books. He told me he had had an antique furniture shop, but like many another had been forced because of the great depression to close his doors, hence the over-furnished rooms upstairs. It seemed when the last remaining Miss Heyden died, the books by will came into the possession of a woman friend. They were stored for some years in a barn near Bradford where the wind, rain and mice had taken their toll. The Englishman now in possession was engaged in selling them on commission for the owner. Considering that he knew next to nothing of Canadian history, he had done a fairly satisfactory piece of work in sorting them. I named a price which was accepted, and then I turned to the rest of the piles, but try as I would he refused to allow me to examine them. Did he regret this, I sometimes wondered. Shortly after I heard that the books were taken out of his hands on the excuse that he had been slow in disposing of them, and stored elsewhere. From then on a few "Heyden" books found their way into the market through other channels. I was fortunate in the lot that came to me, but I never knew what I missed by not being allowed to see the others.

I thoroughly enjoyed examining and cataloguing this collection. They were truly Canadian, and chiefly dealt with Upper Canada at a time when the history of the country was in the making.

Diaries should give the best picture of the times in which they are written, but often they are cruelly disappointing. There are unfortunately few like Pepys and Mrs. Simcoe among the diarists. It was my good fortune to find in the Heyden Library a shining exception to this all too frequent dullness. This one enlivened an otherwise dreary journey for me.

In February, 1933, I had to make a quick trip to Montreal on business. The fast six-hour journey makes me impatient—it does not seem worth while to settle down to enjoy a long book and at that season the scenery is dreary and monotonous. This day, to while away the time, I had packed a small leather-bound, handwritten book which I had found in the Heyden Library. It seemed to be a sort of diary. It was so clearly written that I felt it would be no strain to read it on my journey. By the time I had finished the first page I felt a "wild surmise," for in my hand was a day by day journal of a journey from Montreal to York in February 1817. Now, first-hand accounts of the country at this period are few and far between. This was not only a detailed description of what the traveller saw and felt but the writer himself was a highly intelligent man. Charles Fothergill, the diarist, before coming to Canada in 1816, had written a work called *The Wanderer or a Collection of Original Tales,* and was an ornithologist of some reputation. He had travelled extensively in the British Isles and had come to Canada for further study, the results of which were to have been compiled and published under the title *Memoirs and Illustrations of the Natural History of the British Empire,* but this was never completed.

Seated in my warm, fast-moving train, I read the account of the traveller's long and perilous journey through an unknown country in the depths of winter one hundred and sixteen years earlier. The account began with the first day out from Montreal when he encountered the light-hearted unpredictable French-Canadian drivers in their caleches who, with carefree abandon, drove on whichever side of the road pleased their fancy. Often he was forced by the snowdrifts on the main road to find a way over the frozen river. He was well supplied with English gold which gave him some anxiety as the villages became less frequent and the inns by the roadside less inviting. The war of 1812-1815 had awakened an interest in Canada in the breasts of an undesirable element in the population of New York State, and at the end of hostilities many of these rough characters had established themselves as innkeepers along the border roads. Several times after inspecting the boisterous hospitality offered him, he preferred to drive on into the night with the hope of finding a better night's lodging in some wayside house. As he drove he observed the few signs of bird life and the nature of the country, and with the methodical habits of a confirmed diarist jotted them down at night. By the time he reached Port Hope, or Smith's Creek, as it then was called, in spite of the hardships of the journey, he had become enamoured of Upper Canada. A talk with a chance acquaintance in the village induced him to take a side trip to the back country. When they arrived at Rice Lake it was a brilliant winter day. The beauty and stillness of the scene took possession of him and he determined to return there some day and make it his home. This he did when he built his hunting lodge known as Castle Fothergill on a point on the west side of the mouth of the Otonabee River.

But on this journey his object was to reach York. As I read I was excited at the thought that now I was to read a first-hand account of York by a stranger with a ready pen. Alas, I was doomed to disappointment. As he paused on the high land to the east of the little town he abruptly ended his journal with the words, "I saw York, a mean low lying site!" Others too had thus described it, and perhaps Fothergill, the keen observer, found less to interest him in the straggling settlement than in the unspoiled countryside. There was a short additional diary of a visit to Niagara Falls where he observed eagles and other birds; he ends the account with the statement that for £100 he could have bought Table Rock and ten surrounding acres. Many journals and diaries of Fothergill, chiefly on natural history, have come to light in the last few years.

I was induced to part with the diary to a friend who proposed to publish it. Unfortunately for posterity he has not done so yet. To those who would like to know more about Charles Fothergill I would recommend reading an excellent article on him by Dr. James Baillie, entitled *Charles Fothergill, 1782-1840.* This appeared in the *Canadian Historical Review,* Vol. XXV, Dec. 1944, and it records all that is known of him and sums it up thus: "In addition to being a legislator, King's Printer, Magistrate, and holder of several other public offices, Fothergill was a newspaper publisher, an artist, and one of the first individuals to make studies of the Natural History of the province." Dr. Baillie has been most industrious in his search for information about this talented Canadian, and it is hoped the biography of Fothergill on which he has been working for some time will appear in the not too distant future.

Through the purchase of the Heyden Library I had another interesting experience which has remained vividly in my memory. Coincidence plays a part in everyone's life, but I am firmly convinced that bookmen have more than their share of this curious phenomenon. We never lose our sense of wonder and often with it comes a feeling of accomplishment. Coincidence was a common occurrence in the Book Room and invariably it gave a little fillip to our labours.

A personable young man wandered into my office one day in search of material to help him complete his thesis on the life of his illustrious ancestor, the Hon. Robert Baldwin. He was a direct descendant, he told me, and added, "If you ever come across any letters of Robert Baldwin, I wish you would let me know." I am afraid I replied in the stock phrase, "Now you're asking me!" After all, it was about ninety years since Baldwin died and it was most unlikely that there would be letters in private hands which would come my way.

Three weeks after this conversation I was in possession of the Heyden Library and there among the manuscript material a bundle of about twelve Baldwin letters came to light.

I called up my young friend and asked him to drop in to see me. We chatted for a little while about his work and then I said, "I think I have something you would like," as I put the letters on the table before him. His face was a study in incredulity, turning quickly to delight as he saw the importance of the find. Perhaps I should have seen that these letters were placed in official safe-keeping, but the dealer has to make a choice sometimes between the personal and the impersonal and this time I had no hesitation.

Of the many valuable books in the Heyden Library a few titles stand out vividly in my memory for they were the first copies of them I had ever seen, and for that reason, I suppose, I catalogued them extravagantly. One of these was Robert Gourlay's *Statistical Account of Upper Canada Compiled with a View to a Grand System of Emigration. London 1822, 2 Vols. Maps and Charts.* Also *General Introduction* to the above. This curious work is followed in my catalogue by a quotation from Gagnon's *Essai de Bibliographie Canadienne* which I think gives the most concise account of this curious man.

Gourlay, qui avait des idées politiques quelque peu avancées pour cette époque, porta ombrage au family compact, qui avait alors la haute main sur les affaires du Haut-Canada et il fût emprisonné comme alien, quoiqu'il fût un highlander pure race. Il écrit beaucoup de chaleur. Les "Sketches of Canada" contenus dans cet ouvrage furent, dit-on, écrites par Barnabas Bidwell, alors, maître d'école à Bath, Ont., le père de Marshall Spring Bidwell, qui fût orateur de la chambre du Haut-Canada.

The two main volumes are thick and contain a curious collection of essays and dissertations, arranged with little regard for sequence. They are the outpourings of a clever though eccentric mind. Later I was fortunate in finding some numbers of his curious autobiography entitled *The Banished Briton, and Neptunian, Boston 1843.* The *Statistical Account* appears several times in my catalogues up to about 1940 and then vanishes completely.

Another *Statistical Account of Upper Canada* I found for the first time, but a very different one, was Dr. William Dunlop's little book, published in London in 1832. Someone describes it as "full of information of all kinds, full of reading, full of sagacity, full of humour." In his preface Dunlop says he was so pestered with requests from the old country on life in Canada that in desperation he sat down and wrote this little book. It is and has been for some time scarce and was usually snapped up so eagerly by my customers that I had no time to read it from cover to cover myself. At last I secreted a copy and enjoyed a leisurely hour or so with the sporting doctor. It is in reality chiefly an account of the sport to be found in the Huron tract of Upper Canada, mixed with a minimum of dry statistics. It makes lively reading. There were, too, in the Heyden collection, bundles of early Toronto Almanacs, pamphlets on and by William Lyon Mackenzie; a book on the Canada Company by A. Picken from documents furnished by John Galt, and Galt's own book *The Canadas: etc. London, 1836.* I could continue this list with nostalgic enjoyment to myself, but I fear weariness to my reader. Looking back at my early catalogues, I now know I was extremely fortunate in having this valuable collection come into my hands. If it had come later it would probably have brought me more in monetary reward but I should have missed the incentive to buckle down and study the background from which it came.

In the summer of 1929 I closed the doors of the Book Room for six weeks and with my children took the train for Quebec. This was to be the last visit of the many I had paid to the beautiful old house belonging to the Neilson family, known as "Corsock." Of Scots-French origin, the Neilsons for three generations had lived in this house. It was filled with rare and beautiful furniture, pictures and china, and had a collection of *objets d'art* of the greatest historic interest. Although the house is still standing, I write of it in the past tense for it is now empty of its treasures which, alas, are widely scattered.

"Corsock" was a country house on the St. Louis road, about five miles from the outskirts of Quebec City and, on the other side, three miles from the historic village of Cap Rouge. The house was on rising ground and had a magnificent view over the St. Lawrence River to the distant mountains of Maine. Land on both sides of the St. Louis road belonged to the estate, reaching to the shores of the river. When I first visited the Neilsons as a young girl we used to take picnics to a smugglers' cave deep in the steep cliffs. There we could see traces on the flat rocks where stolen silver had been melted down by the robbers. There were fine woods then to the edge of the cliffs. These woods were later swept away to make shunting space for the railway which was to lead to the great Quebec Bridge. I saw the first bridge begun, to be abandoned after the disastrous collapse on the other side of the river, and arrived the day after the second tragic occasion when the first middle span of the new bridge crashed into the river before the amazed and horrified gaze of the crowds that lined the shore. I shall always remember the sense of deep mourning which prevailed in the countryside for days after the accident. No one spoke of what had happened. They seemed stunned with grief. The next year on the same date, but entirely without fanfare, the second middle span was successfully lifted into place by exactly the same method as the engineers had devised for the erection of the first. I write of this occurrence because the Neilsons' house had been a great centre for the engineers and their families during the years of the building of the bridge, and we often took our afternoon walk, about three-quarters of a mile, to see how the work progressed.

But my story has to do with the library at "Corsock" where I spent many happy hours with Colonel Neilson. How often I have wished since that I had taken notes of the stories he told me about the books, the pictures, the arms and other historic relics.

To give a complete picture of the surroundings it is necessary to tell some details of the lives of the three men who preserved and valued these possessions.

John Neilson was born in Scotland in 1776 and died in Quebec in 1848. When fourteen years of age he was sent to Canada and put under the charge of his elder brother Samuel, who had just succeeded his uncle, William Brown (Canada's first printer) as proprietor and editor of the *Quebec Gazette*. On reaching twenty-one John assumed the direction of the paper, from which time it became an important factor in the development of the Province of Lower Canada. The youthful editor took a deep interest in politics, later resigning his post to enter the Assembly and throughout the stormy period which followed until the union of the provinces in 1841. A contemporary says, "Mr. Neilson's conduct was marked by firmness and impartiality and by that spirit of justice which was part of his individual character." Three times he was chosen as a delegate from the Quebec district to present petitions to the Imperial Parliament, the first time in company with the Hon. Louis Papineau. During the Rebellion of 1837-1838 he stood firmly for his loyal principles and "steadily maintained that the mass of the French-Canadians were untainted by disloyalty and disaffection."

John Neilson married a daughter of the old French-Canadian family of Hubert, through whom his children inherited the Seigneury of Hubert and many interesting possessions. That Mr. Neilson took a deep and practical interest in the welfare and improvement of the province is evident in his library—books and pamphlets on roadmaking, penitentiaries, law, maps and surveys, public health, etc., all of which found a place in his collection. His well-thumbed row of classics was quiet evidence of the way in which this remarkable man spent his hours of relaxation.

The Hon. John Neilson's eldest son, also John, was quite unlike his father. He was an engineer and surveyor and spent a great deal of his time in remote parts of Quebec and down the St. Lawrence River as far as Labrador and Newfoundland. He was an ardent ornithologist and left valuable, though not orderly records of his observations. Either he took little interest in politics, or growing up in a less turbulent time than his father, he was willing to let others govern. There is not much evidence that he added to the already considerable collection of books, though he may have been responsible for the maps and the books on wild life.

Fortunately for posterity his son, J. L. Hubert Neilson, was well aware of the value of the possessions he inherited. He was born in 1846 and died at "Corsock" in 1924. He studied medicine at Laval and became a surgeon in the Canadian Army, and served during the Fenian Raid of 1870, and in the Red River Expedition. Of the latter he told me of the astonishment and dismay of soldiers when they reached Fort Garry to find the rebels gone, their half-eaten breakfast still on the table. There was another story of his Red River service which he told with great gusto. An Indian chief, whether Cree or Blackfoot I do not know, came to consult him about his health. The Colonel prescribed a dose of Seidlitz powders, and either forgot to tell his patient to mix the two powders before swallowing or felt that the Indian would be more impressed with something really startling. The chief proceeded to take the blue and white powders one after the other with the most spectacular results, the effervescent gas coming out of his eyes, ears, nose and mouth. He was much impressed and rewarded the Colonel by giving him the most magnificent Indian costume I have ever seen. The elaborately embroidered leather coat, the feathered headgear, leggings and moccasins hung in a prominent place in the hall of "Corsock" for many years. He was present as a Red Cross surgeon in Serbia during the Russo-Turkish war of 1878 and was with the Canadian voyageurs in the Soudan Expedition of 1894-1895 under General Butler. For this he added to his other honours the Order of St. John of Jerusalem. He was always thankful that he did not smoke, he told me, when he saw what the men suffered without tobacco during the long marches over the deserts. He spent some years at Kingston with "A" and "B" Batteries of the R.C.A., and finally was appointed Director-General of Medical Services at Ottawa. In 1903 he retired to take possession of his grandfather's estate. From then on he lived the life of a country gentleman, walking or snowshoeing over his extensive property, reading, and writing articles for the Literary and Historical Society of Quebec and entertaining callers from all over the world. He had great charm of manner, and was modest about his attainments, though always willing to tell tales of his varied life, if drawn out. I have very tender recollections of this distinguished soldier, connoisseur, and raconteur. Completely bilingual, of course, he had a voice no one ever forgot. On the whole, I think, he was more French than English, though in him the two races were delightfully combined.

During the early years of his retirement he devoted himself to the task of sorting and cataloguing his library, with a view to disposing of it where it would be preserved. He had no direct heirs and knew that it was his task to make wise arrangements so that future historians could have access to it.

No printed list of the Neilson books was ever made, unfortunately, except those which appeared in my catalogues, especially No. 3, but even there they are not distinguishable from others. It is known, however, that the bulk of them went to the Library of the Sulpicians in Montreal. There are, too, a number of them in the Dominion Archives, but I am told by the present Archivist that there is no collection known as the Neilson Library. A small Neilson pamphlet used to turn up from time to time called "Notes on two Jesuit Manuscripts belonging to the estate of the late Hon. John Neilson of Quebec, by l'Abbé Sasserville and Dr. John Gilmay Shea and edited by Geo. M. Fairchild, New York 1887."

I was curious to know what had become of these manuscripts and eventually heard on good authority that one had been sold to J. Pierpont Morgan and the other was given to the Jesuits of Montreal, where it probably still enriches the holdings in the archives of that institution.

The complete file of the *Quebec Gazette* which covers the period 1764 to 1874 was one of the most valuable possessions of the Neilson library. Although I know this file existed, I have never been able to trace its final destination.

Evidently the fear of fire had driven the owners of "Corsock" at some period to build, outside the house proper, a small house known as the Book Room. Here no doubt the valuable books were kept until the final disposal of them. But for some years, as I remember it, the place had been used as a granary, or at least the outer room had held bags of chicken feed. The inside rooms were still lined with bookshelves and on these was a miscellaneous collection of old periodicals, reports, pamphlets, and books. Mice and chickens had found access to the neglected building and had scratched and nibbled at the contents. Five years before my visit of 1928 Colonel Neilson had died and the lovely old place had begun to show signs of neglect. I asked if I might be allowed to examine the tattered remains in the Book Room and was told to take what I wanted as the place had to be cleared out to allow more room for grain and tools. There were bundles of "exchanges" from publishers in Canada and the United States which had been sent to the Gazette offices nearly a century before—periodicals and newspapers, many of which had started hopefully only to come to an abrupt end owing to the failure of subscribers to continue to pay their subscriptions. How often had I seen this sad notice at the end of a year's run, "Our last number owing to the nonsupport of subscribers." Others I found had successfully weathered the first few years and had become well-established and influential papers in both countries. There were also handbills and political pamphlets and books on typography, all of intense interest to the present-day collector and historian. It was hard and dusty work and I did not take time then to examine and sort them. They were due to be destroyed and I was happy to have arrived in time to bundle them into cartons and to ship them to that other Book Room in faraway Ontario.

I was particularly fond of pamphlets and was fortunate in the early days of my book buying to acquire a remarkable number of valuable ones. After the war fewer and fewer came to light, perhaps due to the recklessness of the paper collections during those heart-breaking years.

In the older Disraeli's now almost forgotten book, *The Amenities of Literature,* is a succinct description of the value of pamphlets: "We must consider pamphlets wholly in a political view, their circuit is boundless, holding all the world of man, they enter into every object of human interest. The silent revolution in manners, language, habit, are there to be traced; and indeed, it is in the multiplicity of pamphlets on a particular topic, or object, which appear at a particular period, that offer the truest picture of public opinion."

In looking through the catalogue in which I listed many of the collection I found at "Corsock," I see several that I think are worth recording here.

Among others the *Quebec Magazine for May 1793, vol. 2, No. 14. Printed by John Neilson.* With this very scarce paper is an estimate, written in ink, of the annual expense of publishing a monthly magazine in English and French, of 56 pages, each month for 300 subscribers at $3 per year. The estimates are given in detail and calculated in £:s:d. This was the first magazine published in Canada. There was with this a letter from a subscriber (a publisher of an unsuccessful paper) in Newfoundland, asking to have the magazine as soon as possible as they had no news of the outside world from November to April—dated 1795 and signed W. M. Kurd.

The pamphlets covered the period from the Revolutionary War to the arrival of Durham.

American against Liberty, or an Essay on the Nature and Principles of True Freedom, showing that the Design and Conduct of the Americans, tend only to Tyranny and Slavery. London 1775.

Dalrymple, Sir John. *Address of the People of Great Britain to the Inhabitants of America. London 1775.*

These were distributed in America—apparently to co-operate with a late conciliatory resolution of the House of Commons. This pamphlet belonged to the Hon. J. Neilson, and is marked with great vigour, probably by him.

And another by J. A. Roebuck who, under a bill of the Assembly of Lower Canada, of 1835, was named "Agent of the Province." This one reads: "Remarks on the Proposed Union of the Canadas, 1822. But not published until 1835 in Quebec."

It is difficult to choose from the rich fare I was able to spread before my customers in my third catalogue. I now realize it was not an easy task for an ignorant young bookseller to attempt. It seems to have taken all winter to accomplish it for the catalogue is dated Spring, 1930.

It was a sad farewell for me when the time came to leave Quebec for home. I knew I should never see again the old house as I had known it for more than twenty-five years. I thought of my arrival as a girl of eighteen, fresh from school, with my first ball dress packed in my trunk, ready for the August festivities with which Quebec society greeted the coming of the British fleet in North American waters. That year the flagship was H.M.S. *Ariadne,* and the two cruisers *Tribune* and *Retribution,* and a French man-of-war. There was a military and naval ball at the Citadel to which I went with Colonel Neilson, resplendent in uniform and breast aglow with numerous medals, and with his much-beloved wife. The Governor-General, Lord Minto, was there, and he and Lady Minto showed a good deal of impatience with the ineptness of their partners in the opening set of "Lancers," with which every official ball was begun. It was a warm August night and we strolled between the dances on the battlements and looked down on the ships which swung at anchor, gaily outlined in electric lights to the water's edge.

What a contrast to my departure now. It was always hard to say good-bye to the mountains of Quebec and doubly so this time. Had I not had my two lively children with me my heart would have been heavy indeed. On my doorstep, when I reached home, were ten large cartons of books and pamphlets—I had no time to mope.

It is one thing to buy accumulations of books as I had been doing up to now and quite another to be offered a collector's library. In the former, as a rule, no one hand and mind have been at work to bring all the books together; they, therefore, yield many unexpected finds, and in truth are rather exciting to handle. But when one person has, perhaps over many years, devoted himself to collecting all he can find on one or more subjects, it is an education in itself to sort and catalogue such a library.

One such collection came my way, with very little effort on my part. I was asked to look at a library which had been in storage for many years. It filled a good-sized room from floor to ceiling and was not very easy to examine. The books were tied up very securely in bundles of about one and a half feet high. The cord with which they were tied was firm, though soft, and did not, fortunately, cut into the books. I took my small son along to help move the bundles so that I could get some idea of the material that was in it. This time it was summer and hot and we toiled at the work for about three hours and had only managed to examine about a third of it. It looked extremely good. I asked what the owners wanted for it and agreed to their price and the collection was mine. It arrived in two truck loads, and taxed my storage room to the limits. Would that all other libraries were in such good condition, contained so rich a store, and were so easily handled! For months I read nothing else than the books and pamphlets of this collection. Night after night I chose a bundle and took it upstairs for bedside reading. I learned more from it than from any other collection of books I ever bought, and I also learned something of the mind and character of him who had brought together all these records of the past. Charles Canniff James, whose collection it was, died in 1916 in his early fifties due, it was said, to overwork in the organization of Ontario's agricultural contribution during the first Great War. As I sorted and catalogued the books and papers I was saddened to think he did not live to old age when he could have enjoyed the fruits of his years of collecting. The only consolation one can find on these occasions is the knowledge that they go mostly into the hands of others who value them.

By 1932 I had acquired a really good stock of books and that spring had issued my seventh catalogue.

Among my letters about this time I received a communication from the American Library Association, asking me if I would consider taking a booth at their annual meeting which was to be held that year in Montreal.

I had done practically no advertising so far but was quite well known to many of the librarians of the American universities and institutions, and this seemed a good opportunity to meet them as well as some of my clients in Montreal. I had at that time far more collectors in Montreal and Quebec than I had in Toronto. The rent of the booth did not seem high and I suppose I was ready for a new experience outside the Book Room.

The books were to be arranged all round the large banquet hall of the Windsor Hotel. Publishers from all over the United States and the leading ones in Canada, all from Toronto, had taken booths. I was the only antiquarian bookseller in that great company and a very inexperienced one at that. I bought some pretty clothes, for it was to be in May, packed a big carton of my most outstanding books, and notified some of my bookish friends that I was coming to Montreal for a week, and asked them to look me up.

We arrived on a Monday morning and the bustle and activity in the great hall was terrific. I had arranged for some bookcases to be in my booth and a table or two. My old books looked very dull merchandise beside the gay dust wrappers on the bookshelves and tables of my neighbours. The only new books I had to show were a cluster of dummy volumes of the Encyclopaedia of Canada which was due to be published in a short time. This was in the hands of a small printing firm known as "The University Associates" and the salesman was a very friendly and aggressive personality, and took in most of the orders.

In spite of the undoubted fact that the depression was getting deeper and deeper, a great throng of librarians attended the meeting, chiefly I think from the United States. There were meetings all day in other parts of the hotel and at McGill University and, in between sessions, groups wandered into the banquet hall to examine the displays of the publishers. Each of us had his name on a placard over his booth and I had my share of inquiries. In the evening the book-loving public turned up, for it was a book fair such as Montreal had never before seen. Many of my collectors came to have a talk and I thoroughly enjoyed it, for I am convinced that by and large book collectors are among the most delightful people one can meet.

The next booth to mine was occupied by a German firm from New York. I cannot now recall the name, but the children's books they displayed were the most attractive I have ever seen. There were three young women in charge who told me they had been in New York a year and adored it, but they would soon return to Germany as their visas had expired. I asked them if they would continue to work with their firm, but they said unfortunately, being married women, they would not be allowed to work. This was a year before Hitler seized power, so it could not be laid at his door, but Germany was in the throes of distress and only unmarried women were permitted to work. These young women interested me because I knew they had grown up during the decade after the war when the youth of Germany was struggling to educate itself and the teachers in schools and universities were handicapped for want of money to buy books. I had received pathetic letters from a professor who had spent a year in Canada and was anxious, if possible, to build up a working collection of Canadian literature for his students. He was quite frank in telling me that he and his students hoped gradually to pay me for the books I sent. For two years small amounts came by special permits and then suddenly stopped. I wrote it off as a trifling bad debt, though I still felt it could not be the fault of the professor. Two or three years later came a letter from one of his students telling me that he had died suddenly at the time the money had ceased to come. His former students were heartbroken at losing him and as a memorial were paying the money still owing and ordering a further lot of books to complete the collection they called after him.

Not one French-Canadian publisher was represented at this important gathering, neither were there any Montreal booksellers. Many librarians asked me where they could get a current French book to take home as a memento of their visit. I was sorry I had none to offer but was able to tell them of a few shops in the city which would probably have what they wanted. This seemed a strange situation in a predominantly French city. In the twenty years since this event many French publishers have come to the fore and now have much to offer.

At the end of the week I had a note book full of addresses of institutes of learning in the United States, all, it seemed, with plenty of funds for book buying. This was a most satisfactory outlook in spite of general forebodings. Before leaving for home I drove out of Montreal for a brief holiday in the lovely Laurentians. I remarked to my host that I hoped nothing would happen to the United States of America. His smile was rather wan. Well, nothing did happen just then and fortunately I was well established when the American banks, one after the other, closed their doors and the appropriations of many of their educational institutions were cut to a discouraging minimum.

3. Catalogues and Bibliographies—Required Reading

Study what you most affect.
—Shakespeare.

I can think of no duller reading than catalogues and bibliographies for those outside the inner circle of collectors, librarians and booksellers. I had not been long in the trade when I realized that such books were "required reading" for me although previously I hardly knew of their existence. It speaks well for their innate charm that I came to depend on them and to even enjoy them.

In an old book called *The Book Fancier or the Romance of Book Collecting,* Percy Fitzgerald has some pleasant things to say about book dealers and although he insists, as others have before and after him, in calling us *quaint,* we must forgive him for he says, "the 'old book' dealers of London are an interesting class, all knowing their business thoroughly. The amount of bibliographical lore they acquire and spend over their catalogues is often surprising." He goes on to say, "Most *litterateurs* will admit they always find in good catalogues agreeable and piquant reading." These observations form a preface to some unavoidable technical observations on the subjects at the head of this chapter.

It was possible in the first years of my business life to accumulate some of the best catalogues that were ever put out by the book dealers of the British Isles. The great names of Maggs, Stevens Sons and Styles, Edwards, the Museum Book Shop, Quarich, and many others became familiar to me through their scholarly publications. All of them, regardless of printing cost, annotated each title, not only with minute description of the copy offered but with learned notes on its contents and accurate details of any deviations from other editions. I found these volumes, some running over a thousand pages, of immense value when trying to trace editions and prices of rare Canadiana.

The American catalogues were helpful, though not to the same degree, the sections on Canada being as a general rule rather brief. The exception to this rule was the long run of fine catalogues issued by Goodspeed's Book Shop in Boston. I am sorry that during those busy years I never had the opportunity to visit their shop at 12 Beacon Street. While I was planning to write this account of my book selling career, I read with great pleasure Charles E. Goodspeed's book called *Experiences of an American Book Seller*. Boston, 1937.

Canadian book catalogues were a fairly new venture when I began, except for the veterans in the trade, such as Georges Ducharme and Albert Britnell (Roy's father). I see the names of Lauren and Douglas among my pile of old catalogues. These two issued a few interesting lists, but died young, and left the field to Georges Ducharme, Lee Pritzker, Harold Creassor, John Forsyth and myself, for the next two decades.

The antiquarian bookseller must be familiar with the great bibliographies, compiled by scholars with great industry and care, for they are his invaluable tools.

Information on Canadian books is widely scattered through many publications, but gradually the searcher learns which ones are best suited to his needs.

I was always proud of my collection of bibliographies and nothing would induce me to part with them. They were the text books of my self-imposed course of study, from which I never graduated.

Skipping over such well-known names as Faribault, Morgan and Dionne, I shall confine myself to relating my experience with the ones I relied on most.

In 1886 William Kingsford issued a little book called *Canadian Archaeology*, and in 1892 a second one called *The Early Bibliography of Ontario.* These small books were written in the form of essays and told the story of certain early publications in Upper Canada. When I was fortunate enough to come across copies of early printing it was possible through these little books to place them in their proper setting. At the period when the Kingsford books were published nearly seventy years ago, their appeal must have been limited to a few scholars. And yet there seem to have been quite large editions issued, for they still turn up in unexpected places. In the course of my career I accumulated quite a supply.

Phileas Gagnon's *Essai Bibliographie Canadienne* was always beside me when I was preparing a catalogue. Two volumes were issued, but I relied upon the first almost entirely. This work is not an impersonal list of Canadian publications but the record of one man's library, collected over many years. There are 700 pages and 5,018 entries, with numerous facsimiles of title pages, and most endearing of all are the annotations. Gagnon loved his books and knew the contents of most of them. Sometimes a little story is told about his copy, or a sentence or two is picked out of the book to illustrate its worth. He occasionally even tells how much he paid for his copy, an unheard of descent to the mundane, in a bibliography. While most of the titles are French ones, there are quite enough in both languages to make it extremely useful to any student of Canadiana.

Towards the end of his life Gagnon disposed of his unique collection to the city of Montreal.

Two small bibliographies which I found very useful are: C. C. James' *Bibliography of Canadian Poetry to 1899* and L. E. Horning and L. Burpee's *Bibliography of Canadian Fiction to 1905.* A great deal of research was needed to compile these lists. The brief biographical notes add much to their usefulness and it is quite a triumph to come across a slim book of poems, or a worn work of fiction which is not recorded in them.

In 1934 the great volume appeared which was a gift from the gods to librarians and booksellers. After years of work the Toronto Public Library, under the able editorship of Miss F. M. Staton and Miss Marie Tremaine, issued *A Bibliography of Canadiana, being items in the Public Library of Toronto, Canada, relating to the early history of development of Canada.*

This splendid work, catalogued chronologically the treasures housed in the Library from the earliest records to the year of Confederation, 1867. Few suspected that Toronto possessed such a rich store. Again, this volume, like Gagnon's, arouses our admiration by bringing to light facts of intense interest on a vast number of the books. It was quite a triumph for a bookseller when cataloguing a book to be able to add the magic words, "Not in Staton and Tremaine." This meant it was indeed rare.

For her skilled work and zeal in listing 4,646 pieces and bringing this book to such perfection Miss Tremaine was awarded a grant and two years' leave of absence from the

Library in order to pursue another ambitious project, that of listing the Canadian imprints before 1800.

Canadian incunabula is scattered throughout eastern Canada and the United States, in numerous large and small libraries, and it was a difficult task requiring infinite patience. In 1952 Miss Tremaine published the results of this painstaking hunt under the title, *A Bibliography of Canadian Imprints, 1751-1800.*

To merely list Canadian printing in its "swaddling clothes" is a great accomplishment, but both scholars and booksellers are indebted to the author for her revealing annotations, historical notes on the early printing houses, the biographies of the printers, references to private holdings of imprints and a wealth of other detail on the subject. Those who are interested in this subject will find much to entertain them in the introduction of Marie Tremaine's bibliography. She says,

> The craft of printing appeared very late in the Canadian scene . . . Almanacs were the colonial printer's staple . . . the 18th century thriller was the "confession," or "true story" of a man about to be hanged usually for theft or murder . . . Many proclamations, orders-in-council and regulations were printed . . . surprisingly few of the items printed relate directly to industry . . . poetry, drama, and belles-lettres appeared hardly at all from the earliest Canadian presses . . . The first substantial volume produced in Quebec was a Roman Catholic catechism in 1765 . . . and Protestant devotional books were conspicuously lacking in early printing in Quebec.

Only those who have a burning enthusiasm for the subject will, I suppose, read the book item by item, but to dip into it here and there will enlarge one's understanding of the long and painful road travelled by the courageous early printers.

The Royal Empire Society of London, England, was one of my favourite customers from the time I put out my first catalogue. The Society, when first established, was called the Royal Colonial Institute, and had at that time begun to build up a library on Britain's overseas possessions. I enjoyed my contacts with the courteous and, I must add, leisurely ways of the librarians. Their letters were always polite and considerate and bespoke the unhurried atmosphere of the British Isles.

The great catalogue volumes of the Royal Empire Society had been in preparation for many years and it was my good fortune to have been in business only four years when the third volume came out in 1932. This one forms a geographical unit confined to Canada and its provinces, Newfoundland, the West Indies and Colonial United States. The Canadian Section not only includes most of the rarer books on exploration and development, but it has an almost complete collection of Parliamentary documents, including mining, geology, etc., and it is especially rich in books and reports on the native races. At first I found the large volume a little difficult to use since its cataloguing arrangement is unusual. Later I found it most useful when I discovered that all the contents of our learned societies' transactions were listed in detail. For instance, the long run of the Ontario Archaeological Reports has no general index. Here the contents of each report in detail are given chronologically. I had the sale of this important catalogue in Canada. When the librarian, Mr. Evans Lewen, kindly pointed out to me that my four catalogues were listed in it, I felt my first pleasant glow of accomplishment.

The war came and part of this famous library was lost by bombing. How great the loss was I never knew exactly, but years after I was asked by the librarian for a complete run of the *Canadian Magazine* "which has been lost through bombing."

This periodical began publication in 1893 and appeared

monthly in the same format till 1922. It was, therefore, quite a problem thirty years later to collect a set, but it is the bookseller's pride not to fail his old clients. In a short time I had purchased about a ton of this interesting periodical from my old friend and valued colleague, Mr. J. W. Worden, who had been collecting them for years. When the collection was delivered, it was spread over the entire floor of one of my office rooms, almost knee high. Hundreds of numbers had to be sorted—no easy task. Why editors of magazines, or whoever is responsible, like to vary the corner in which to put the date remains a mystery. The *Canadian Magazine* during these years was a remarkable example of temperamental dating. There were years when the covers took on a particularly attractive appearance—a Canadian painting being reproduced in colour each month—and then the date was completely forgotten, except possibly on the spine which was the first part to disappear. My daughter was working with me by the time I received this order and as we stood surveying the task before us one of our favourite customers appeared at our office door. We explained the reason for the cluttered condition of our floor and the job that lay before us. "I'd love to help," he said, "I have nothing particular to do tomorrow if you can wait till then." This was too good an offer to refuse and with instructions to come in old clothes he departed. As good as his word he returned and worked steadily all day until dusty, but triumphant, he and my daughter displayed forty-four volumes, lacking only five numbers to make the file complete. The *Canadian Magazine,* for the first twenty-two years of its existence, was truly devoted to the Canadian scene. The authors were for the most part Canadian and they wrote of our music, our art and literature, our outdoor life and our military exploits. Take, for example, the copy of January, 1898, and you may read "The Castle of St. Louis," by J. M. Lemoine, illustrated from old prints; "Canada's Call to the Empire," by Colonel Vincent; "Colonial Clubs," by Ernest Heaton; "The Alaska Boundary Question," by R. N. Gosnell; "Hockey in the Canadian North West," by H. J. Woodside, with drawings by F. H. Brigden; and to show that history does repeat itself, a serious article with graphs and statistics called "The Fall in Prices and the Effect on Canada." There is plenty of atmosphere of the period in these old periodicals for future generations. I know of one novelist who was gathering material for a Canadian novel of the span of years from 1890 to 1910, and found a wealth of material in the articles and illustrations of the *Canadian Magazine.* The advertisements were clipped to keep her correct on fashions in clothes and articles in daily use at the time.

But I must return to the subject of bibliographies.

The reader may well ask what effort has been made to record all the works by Canadian authors since 1900. Only in 1950 was this gap bridged by a bulky volume known as *A Check List of Canadian Publications, 1900-1925,* compiled by Dorothea Tod and Audrey Cordingley, and put out in a temporary form by the Canadian Bibliographical Centre at the Public Archives in Ottawa. This is arranged alphabetically and, while the editors do not claim it is complete, it is a valuable contribution and brings the record up to the issue of the Toronto Public Library's annual catalogues known as *Canadian Catalogue of Books Published in Canada, about Canada, as well as those written by Canadians.*

These small books were issued until 1949 and were extremely useful. In 1951 the work was continued by the Bibliographical Centre at Ottawa. Just for the record, the gap of the year 1950 has never been satisfactorily bridged.

Booksellers not only must have something to sell, but they must know all there is to know of their wares. I found it not only stimulating to myself to have some knowledge of the books I handled, but it was helpful to my clients. Once you have looked up a book in a bibliography you are not likely to forget it.

Gradually I became aware that I was compiling a collection of small bibliographies that did not appear in any of the printed works I so frequently consulted.

A client would ask for a complete run of the *Canadian Parliamentary Companions,* which were later on called *Guides.* I had to know whether these little books were published every year since 1862 when they began. Through a man in Ottawa who made a study of these I was able to get a list. They were not published every year, it appeared. Few publications, it seems, are unable to avoid a sabbatical year. Another useful small bibliography is the one listing *Canadian Literary Periodicals 1789-1900, Tod and Cordingley.* This subject has been since more fully explored and continued in *A Bibliography of Canadian Cultural Periodicals (French and English from Colonial Times to 1950),* compiled by Goggio, Corrigan and Parker. Toronto, 1955. All indices and data on historical societies were filed, and an especially interesting one to me was an annotated list of Illustrated Historical Atlases of the Counties of Ontario. The list I had with infinite trouble compiled myself was succeeded by a more complete one published in the *Ontario Library Review.*

By the time I turned this file over to my successor it contained dozens of invaluable records and hardly a day passed, in a business such as this one, when reference would not be made to it.

Since I write as a bookseller, I must confess that after

absorbing all this information we are still left with the highly important detail of arriving at suitable prices. Here we must use our own judgment and take our chances. I have tried to throw more light on this problem in another chapter.

Habits of twenty-six years' standing are not easily broken. To this day, when opportunity comes, I cannot resist dipping into an old book catalogue or reading the preface of a new bibliography.

4. My Colleagues

Book collecting is mainly a personal affair which begins and ends with life.

—Hazlett.

When I stepped out of my old world into what I thought was a secluded corner of the book trade, I had no idea that I had joined a company not so much of friends as of colleagues. I liked the word for it implied we had one common interest—books—and particularly Canadian books. It was unnecessary in our friendships to know much about each other beyond this bond, and it speaks well for our good nature that we never had a "falling out." We were frank with each other up to a point. We knew instinctively we need not tell each other all our peregrinations, our trials and our triumphs, though there was always plenty of amusing book gossip when we met. I have jotted down some thumbnail sketches of those who most frequently crossed my threshold in person or by letter.

Georges Ducharme's career as a bookman is unique in the annals of antiquarian bookselling in Canada, and I have the happiest recollections of my long association with him. He was head and shoulders above us all in his knowledge of Canadian books, both English and French, but particularly in the realm of valuable French records, and he willingly shared his knowledge with his clients and colleagues. He was generous to a fault and his business ethics were beyond reproach. He was meticulous in answering his large correspondence, for the most part in longhand, and quantities of his familiar bright pink note paper must be found in the files of libraries throughout the United States and Canada.

I have a vivid memory of a visit I made to Montreal especially to call at Librairie Ducharme, 995 rue Saint Laurent, one typical winter day when the mercury hovered around zero. A narrow stair ran up to the second floor of an old building, not too easily found among its neighbours in that undistinguished region. There sat Georges Ducharme comfortably swathed in a heavy sweater coat, beside a huge stove, surrounded by an enormous number of bookshelves which seemed to reach endlessly in a dimly lit vista. Beside him was a large square box in which he kept recorded, on cards, all the books and pamphlets which passed through his hands. There were two more storeys of books above the main office, but as they were not heated even by stoves, only the hardiest Montrealer would venture to inspect them during the long winter months.

Ducharme was born in 1875 and died in 1950, sincerely mourned by collectors of Canadiana as a great bookman. By profession he was a school teacher and had held important posts, as a such, until 1914 when he retired to begin his career as a bookseller and to found the Librairie Ducharme, specializing in Canadian books. His knowledge rapidly became a legend and he was consulted by many as an authority on Canadian incunabula as well as on the latest publication referring to Canada. By 1928 he had issued twenty-six catalogues. Number 27 was the first of his ten catalogues which were alphabetically arranged throughout. These ran from January, 1928, to October, 1930, and contained the prodigious number of 19,569 separate items beginning with "A brief account of the Messien established among the Eskimo on the Coast of Labrador by the church of the Brethren. London, 1774," and ending with "Zouaves Pontificaux de Québec, 1895." All these books and pamphlets are recorded with the utmost correctness as to date and place of publication, number of pages (the introductions being in roman figures), binding, condition and price. I think this is without parallel in the history of priced book catalogues. I am fortunate in the possession of a set of these catalogues which I early realized were valuable and had them bound. It was quite possible, years after these were issued, to ask, for example, for No. 2473—*The Canadian North-West Territories, Dairy Farming, Ranching, Mining 1891—64 p. Map 30c*—and receive it a few days later with a bill for 30c. Mr. Ducharme, through example, taught me the importance of certain business principles; to issue regular catalogues; to answer all correspondence with promptness and courtesy; and not to overlook the potential value of a pamphlet.

Book collectors, librarians and dealers owe to the memory of Georges Ducharme a vast debt of gratitude. He stimulated the taste for collecting Canadian books and raised the dignity of antiquarian book selling in Canada to a peak it never before attained.

No account of my friends and colleagues in the alluring occupation of book selling would be complete without a reference to two outstanding bookmen, Mr. A. V. White and Mr. Fred Ketcheson. Both these men began as ardent collectors of Canadiana with the intention of eventually selling their books when the busy years of their professional life had passed. They had no need then to wonder how they would occupy their leisure hours.

I do not remember the exact date when Mr. White first

found his way to the Book Room door, but I know it was while my children were still young enough to come on the run through the office, whereat Mr. White would smile and say, "What health, what vigour."

By profession Mr. White was a hydro engineer and in his younger days devoted much time to the preparation of reports on the water powers of Canada for the Commission on Conservation, 1910-1921. His most notable report was known as *The Water Powers of British Columbia.* To compile this he spent five years in the far west and being a bookman as well as an engineer, he amassed a vast collection of books and reports bearing on his work. These he catalogued, together with the books he had consulted on every aspect of the history and development of the Province of British Columbia. This valuable bibliography appears at the end of his *Water Powers* report and I recommend it particularly on the interesting subject of the Canadian Pacific Railway. Several times I separated this from the now obsolete report and put it in my catalogue, and it always found a ready buyer.

About 1932 Mr. White retired and from then on devoted most of his waking hours to the accumulation of more books. He filled most of the rooms in his large old-fashioned house; he built shelves in two nearby garages; he stored endless reports in his own and the next-door cellar. He was not content with one copy of each book and pamphlet—he must have all he could lay his hands on. I remember once I had acquired a large quantity of speeches delivered on the hustings by such stalwarts as Laurier, Edward Blake, Mowat and others of that period. There were many copies of each of the speeches and they probably did not appear complete except in this form. Mr. White was fascinated with them and wanted to buy all I had and while I was happy to let him have the lion's share, I thought it better salesmanship to reserve a few.

His intention was to "corner" certain publications with the hope that when the demand arose for them his would be the only source of supply.

Mr. White loved books and to justify his insatiable desire to buy had persuaded himself that they were the best investment he could make for his money. In some ways he was right provided he lived long enough to liquidate his holdings for himself.

From time to time he issued lists though he never let me see them and we did not actually discuss this angle of our relationship. On the other hand he knew that I knew! Occasionally he would arrive with a small bundle of nice books and we would enter into a complicated system of barter. I am still in doubt as to what happened to all those hustings speeches, but I know that on one "corner" he made an excellent guess. To tell this story some explanation is necessary.

There has always been a demand for dictionaries and grammars of the various Indian languages. So much so that it is strange none has been issued by the Department of Indian Affairs (now under Citizenship and Immigration). For instance, the chief grammar and dictionary of the Ojibway language is the very rare work by Bishop Baraga, issued in Montreal in 1879. In my catalogue No. 39 (1939) I listed this with several other unusual books on our Indians. The price for Baraga was $50 and it is certain it has not gone down since then. This all leads up to Mr. White's discovery of a source of supply of Indian dictionaries. He must have had some interest in the Colportage Mission which had its headquarters in Toronto, 202 King Street East, for he arrived there one day to find the place closed up and empty. He was determined to find out what had become of the stock of books which the mission kept for distribution among the Indians. At last he heard they had been bought by some man now living on the outskirts of the city. Off he went and was rewarded by finding among other books a large pile of Ojibway dictionaries and some small primers and hymn books in English and Ojibway. He brought them all home and made a complete corner this time, for I never came across them anywhere else. The "grapevine," which flourishes so congenially in the atmosphere of the book trade, is responsible for these facts while Mr. White maintained his conspiracy of silence. For many years, however, he allowed me to buy the dictionaries from him for which I am grateful. It brought me into contact with Indians, in various walks of life, with trappers, missionaries, teachers, and proprietors of fishing camps, and a section of the general public who curiously enough wanted to be able to converse in Ojibway.

Mr. White was always warmly welcomed in our office. He usually had an amusing story to tell us and even if we had heard it from him before, we laughed heartily for he told it well. He wore his bowler hat at a jaunty angle, suggestive of a sporting inclination which was far from being the case—at least when I knew him. Once he said, "If I had my way, I would take all the girls out of offices and put them in flower gardens." "Oh, Mr. White," I exclaimed in astonishment, "they would be bored to death!"

He had another curious belief, quite as archaic. He believed the world was flat, and that in spite of being an engineer. He must, however, have had some doubts because he devoted a great deal of his time to the study of this problem. He made enquiries all over the world for pictures showing the path of the midnight sun in the Antarctic. He explained there were plenty of pictures, photographs and diagrams of the sun in the Arctic appearing above the horizon and presently dipping again below it, but none of it performing the same arc in the south.

This definitely proved something and he took great pride in the shelf of books he had accumulated on this curious subject.

There was one tense episode in my book-dealing affairs with Mr. White. One day when he dropped into the office I was absorbed in the examination of a new find. The story went that a stenographer in an old law firm in Toronto was helping to sort out and destroy its ancient files, and among other papers of no particular interest she found a bundle of affidavits and letters which bore the date 1838. Attracted by this significant date in Canadian history she asked if she could preserve them and was told they were not wanted and she could do what she liked with them. In the end they reached my hands and the bright girl did not lose in the transaction.

I found they were the affidavits, sworn before the mayor, of those who had taken part in the historic march on Toronto at the instigation of William Lyon Mackenzie on December 7, 1838. There were sworn statements on the behaviour of their leader, highly detrimental; a letter from Colonel Anthony van Egmont, and other first-hand evidence of the way Mackenzie's followers had been misled.

In my enthusiasm I began to describe my find to Mr. White, and while in the midst of this in walked another interesting customer, Mr. C. R. Dent, and I included him in the conversation. Now Mr. Dent had a more than passing interest in the subject for he was the son of John Charles Dent, the author of two outstanding books on the period, *The Story of Upper Canada Rebellion,* 2 vols. 1885, and *The Last Forty Years; Canada since the Union of 1841,* 2 vols. 1882.

Mr. Dent and Mr. White knew each other well and I became aware, to my embarrassment, that they both wanted my collection of twenty-five contemporary Rebellion pieces. As I had not then arrived at a suitable price, I found myself in a difficult position. I longed for the wisdom of Solomon. Suddenly a solution flashed into my mind and I said, "Gentlemen, I shall make two lists of all the items in this collection with the price I want for them. I shall then mail one to each of you by the same post and the person who gets here first shall have them!"

I think the sporting nature of the proposition appealed to them, for they went away together in friendly converse.

A few days later the two letters were ready and with my own hands I posted them. Before nine o'clock the next morning Mr. White was on my doorstep with a cheque for $100 in his hand.

Mr. Dent was pleasant about the affair, confessing that the price was more than he wished to pay, but he hoped Mr. White would allow him to see the collection. As time went on and Mr. White maintained a complete silence on the subject, Mr. Dent became more and more irritated. "I don't think he has even undone the parcel," he exclaimed, and I fear friendly relations became strained. I was rather curious myself to know what Mr. White intended to do with it but refrained from asking. After Mr. White's death some years later, the box was found by his family but it contained no instructions about the valuable contents. I was able to sell it on behalf of his family to the Ontario Department of Archives, a very suitable ultimate resting place.

Second-hand book shops have always been hot beds of book gossip. Mr. White enjoyed his visits to my Book Room, but even more he revelled in the hours spent in the little back room of Mr. Herman's crowded book shop on Yonge Street, just above Gloucester Street.

Mr. Herman was an Austrian, with a background of books in his native country, but it was not till after he had been some years in Canada that he began selling books in a rather pretentious shop on King Street West. He had a gracious and friendly way with his customers, but unfortunately there were not enough of them and his venture was short-lived. Not discouraged, he later took an old shop on Yonge Street, more picturesque and less expensive to maintain. He bought liberally and his shelves soon had that pleasantly overflowing appearance so dear to the heart of book hunters, and his shop became a rendezvous for droppers-in. But just as the tide of mild prosperity was turning in his favour Mr. Herman died suddenly. Mr. White was lost without his congenial companion and this haven. He told me sadly he never passed the empty shop without thinking regretfully of his old friend.

In spite of old age and failing health Mr. White never gave up his lifelong pursuit. He actually continued to order books until the day of his death. It remained for his wife to dispose of his vast collection. This she did with great care and unusual wisdom, by private sale, volume by volume.

My other friend and colleague, who began as a collector and on retirement became a very successful bookseller, was Mr. Fred Ketcheson. He came of pioneer stock, from ancestors who had settled along the north shore of Lake Ontario. Through family traditions and associations it was natural then that he should become interested in things Canadian. Endowed with a keen mind, a remarkably retentive memory and a ready supply of cash, he built up during thirty years or more the most valuable and distinguished collection of books up to that time ever held in private hands in Canada. This statement may be challenged by some who think there are greater collections in French hands. But the French collections seldom included much English, while Mr.

Ketcheson had both, with a preponderance of the rare Upper Canada titles. These last were his first love. I think he retained his interest in them until his death in 1956.

He came to this field of collecting at a time when few others realized its value, and his travels about the country as the representative of the New York Life Insurance Company gave him unusual opportunities to comb the remoter places in his search. Moreover, like Mr. Paul Hahn, he had a "nose" for likely places. He never passed the red flag of an auctioneer without dropping in to look over the tattered display of old cook books and almanacs in a rickety bookcase in the hope of finding an early school book or a pioneer newspaper. But Mr. Ketcheson was equally ready to buy a whole library, if necessary, in order to secure a few small pieces of early printing, and although all is fair in the purchase of books as well as in the pursuit of love and war we, the dealers, sometimes felt a little nettled when we heard about these transactions.

Mr. Ketcheson walked into my office at an opportune moment for us both. I had recently purchased the C. C. James library, a treasure trove of early Upper Canada imprints, from which he could choose, and I needed cash. We exchanged our wares, with much satisfaction on both sides, and considerable enlightenment to me.

Now Mr. Ketcheson did not confine himself to incunabula, Canadian printing in its "swaddling clothes," or his sphere would have been indeed limited. Early in the nineteenth century the field became wider but not wide enough to spoil the sport.

At the same time that Mr. Ketcheson was pursuing the elusive early imprint, he was building up an impressive collection of fine Canadian books on the fur trade, on transportation, naval and military narratives, and local histories—to name only a few of his favourite subjects. He did not, as did Mr. White, deliberately duplicate his books, but if he found a nice copy of a book which he already possessed, at a reasonable price, he bought it and tucked it into the capacious pocket of his greatcoat.

This reminds me of the remark of, I fear, a henpecked client of mine as he regretfully put down a large book, "You see, I can't take home anything that won't go into this pocket."

When Mr. Ketcheson was moved to Montreal by his company, it took two large trucks to transport his library to the large house he was forced to take, and a few years later, on his retirement, back they came in three truck loads. Then he settled down to give his undivided attention to the task to which he had looked forward for so many years. In 1945 he issued the first of his twelve catalogues, each bearing the caption, "selected from my private library." But he did not part with his early printed collection while he lived. Several years after his death this unique library of rare Canadian imprints was sold to Mr. Louis Melzack of Montreal, for a substantial but undisclosed amount.

For many years Mr. Ketcheson had kept track of the trend in prices through watching catalogues and sales so that he did not approach the task of pricing as an amateur. If he was inclined to underprice the more familiar titles because he had many copies of them, he could ask what he liked for his extremely rare titles. Some of my colleagues groused at this invasion into our field, but I maintained that we had no monopoly of the business and that any venture that stimulated the purchase of books in Canada redounded to our advancement. By the time he had issued his twelfth catalogue he had disposed of the bulk of his library, retaining only his unique collection of early imprints. His catalogues, too, are well worth preserving. They are the work of an expert and list many rare and interesting examples of Canadiana.

Among the other collector-dealers who issued catalogues during the past twenty-five years was Mr. Victor Morin of Montreal, the senior of us all by many years and head and shoulders above us all in his knowledge of French-Canadian books.

I soon learned book dealers may be divided into two classes—the movers and the stationary. Mr. John Worden and I belonged to the latter group, I who have never moved and Mr. Worden who had been in the same shop on Yonge Street for at least fifteen years. Mr. Worden was, like Mr. Ducharme, a school teacher by profession. Quite early in his life he took to bookselling and when I first knew him had been at it for a good many years. I do not think it would be possible to mention an English-Canadian book that Mr. Worden did not know. Dates and editions were on the tip of his tongue even though it was years perhaps since he had possessed the book in question. Although he owned a good collection of Canadiana, it was only with the greatest reluctance that he would part with any portion of it, since his real income came from the huge pile of second-hand magazines behind which he sat in his chilly shop. But if you felt in the mood for a pleasant chat on Canadian books, there was no one who was more willing to share his information or to relish your story than Mr. John Worden. Since writing this account Mr. Worden's death has occurred at the age of eighty-three, after a mercifully short illness, leaving his collection of Canadiana undisturbed. His love of his books transcended every other circumstance of his life. This is a solemn thought in our modern world given over, it seems, to monetary gain and comforts.

To the "movers" among us the prize must go to Mr. Lee Pritzker. Our careers ran concurrently. It was during the first few months of the Book Room that Mr. Pritzker came in with a small parcel of books under his arm. Though the first Great War had been over for ten years he was still visibly suffering from the effects of shell shock and shattered nerves, and this condition may have contributed to his restlessness. In spite of spells of ill-health and many moves he built up a good business and was well versed in Canadian books. Like many another in this curious trade, he disliked the grind of sorting, classifying and arranging his stock. It was much more entertaining and sometimes more profitable to follow scents and hunt down new treasures than to reduce the confusion of his office to some semblance of order. Although we had many transactions over the years and always got on well, I remember once we almost came to blows. Our conversation ran something like this:

Pritzker: "I have a room full of material I think you would like to see. Can you come down today?"
Hood: "Is it far away?"
Pritzker: "No."
Hood: "Is it cold?"
Pritzker: "Not so bad."
Hood: "Are the books on shelves?"
Pritzker: "Well, no, but you can see them all right."

So off I went and it led to an unusual find for my customer, Mr. E. J. Salmon, whose collection I had lately become interested in.

Mr. Salmon's specialty was authentic pictures of bygone Toronto in books, on postcards, or actual photographs; the period covered was the last one hundred years, since the introduction of photography. Now Mr. Salmon had an impressively large collection before he came to me for assistance, but it is surprising how the horizon continues to widen with each acquisition.

There are, of course, other people with much the same hobby, but for thoroughness the field must be divided between Mr. T. A. Reed and Mr. Salmon.

But to return to Mr. Pritzker. Off I went to a warehouse on a back street in the centre of the city. How dreary these places can be! This time the books were in a large cupboard into which I could hardly wedge myself. I was a bit annoyed when I stubbed my toe against a heavy box. I leaned down and found it was full of photographic plates. They were cabinet size and each was in a separate envelope on which was printed the subject of the photograph. They were all views of Toronto buildings, parks, docks, railways of sixty to seventy years ago. I became rather suddenly very agreeable and bought the whole three dozen of them.

I have seldom seen a man so pleased as Mr. Salmon was when he saw the treasure trove. He told me he might have picked them up one by one over the years, but to find so many together was a collector's dream come true.

Early in my acquaintance with Mr. Pritzker I learned of his unbounded admiration for Bernard Shaw. This dated back to the years following the first Great War when he was convalescing at the home of Mrs. William Archer, widow of the playwright and critic, and friend of G.B.S. Here he became familiar with stories of his hero which led him to study the Fabian philosophy and later to found the Bernard Shaw Society of Canada, of which he is still President. About a year before Shaw's death he took a trip to England and had the great satisfaction of paying his respects to the famous man.

We, the dealers of Canada, all came to take up our avocation by easy routes compared with that of our late colleague, Mr. Sol Wenroth. All credit to him who became so proficient and acquired such a remarkable instinct for the uncommon and rare. Sol came with his parents from Poland when he was quite a young lad. He had first to learn the language and then with little or no help from his surroundings to develop a taste for literature and art. He spent all his spare time, he once told me, tramping the city streets between the Art Gallery, the Museum and the Public Libraries to study the rare and the beautiful. His instincts told him these books and *objets d'art* would not have been preserved had they not some value and with Semitic sense of monetary values he set out to see what he could find in the great city that was growing so fast around him. Many a public and private collection is the richer through his taste and industry. Well might it be said of him, "I am but a gatherer and dispenser of other men's stuff." (Sir W. Wotton)

It was through Mr. Wenroth that I bought a remarkable collection of letters. A large trunk had been carefully partitioned off, leaving spaces about four inches wide which would just hold a letter folded lengthwise, and each slot was filled to the brim. On examination I found these were the letters received by Sir Alexander Campbell during his term of office as Lieutenant-Governor of Ontario, 1888-1892. It was a period of much development in the province and many prominent men who were involved in new ventures seemed to have taken the Governor into their confidence. Campbell had been meticulous in preserving the letters, and they undoubtedly throw a good deal of light on the time. Dipping into them I found many written by the fathers and grandfathers of my friends and I was sorely tempted to remove some of them for my own amusement. They were, of course, mine to dispose of as I wished, but I am now happy that I left them intact, especially as with the collection came the duplicate letter books of Campbell's replies. Besides there was a large bundle, enclosed in a leather case, of letters from Sir John A. Macdonald. I have examined many of Sir John's letters, for he carried on a prodigious correspondence, and have come to the conclusion that he had a secretary whose handwriting could easily be mistaken for his own, although this may not have been his intention. It is sometimes easy to detect when the colour of the ink is slightly different in the signature.

I told Miss Helen McClung, then acting Archivist, about the collection, and she very wisely bought it for the Department. Her staff at the time was small but she took time to make a calendar of the letters for further reference.

Sol Wenroth unearthed an extraordinary amount of unusual material and placed it to good advantage. He always seemed to have a fat roll of bills with which to buy more, but, he, too, soon become bored with the dull work of sorting piles of stock, with the result that vast quantities of books and pictures piled up in his shop on Yonge Street and elsewhere. Then illness overtook this dynamic man and suddenly we were all shocked to hear that Sol was dead at the age of forty-five. The auction sale of his stock lasted for most of a week. I know of no one else who has taken just his place in the antiquarian community of Toronto and Montreal.

On looking back over the lives of my colleagues whose work, like mine, has been "to see, uncover and wrest from obscurity that which is worth preservation" (Treadwell, slightly adjusted), I feel there has been little public recognition of their skill and industry. Our libraries and museums have benefited vastly by their daring in risking their capital to preserve some treasure often with little certainty that they will get it back. Once, I am happy to say, I found occasion to fight a battle for Mr. Wenroth when I thought he should have received public thanks.

A certain institution had bought from him some unique material. This greatly enhanced the value of their holdings on the same subject, and threw much needed light on important aspects of the work being carried on by one member of the staff. In due course this research worker wrote a paper, on the basis of Mr. Wenroth's find, for a learned publication. As usual at the end of the article appeared a long list of acknowledgments for help given in preparing it. Librarians, archivists, professors and private individuals were politely thanked. But nowhere, either in the article or at the end, was any mention of the person who actually was responsible for finding and preserving the basic material. This seemed to me to be highly unethical and I pointed it out to the writer. He put the blame on the editor of the journal who told him, he said, it was quite unnecessary to make any mention of the "dealer." The inference was that he had been paid for it. I could not resist pointing to the fact that no matter how professional the others might be, they too were only doing their day's work.

5. Reminiscences of Collectors and Book Buyers

Never waste your pity on a Collector.

I FIND IT IMPOSSIBLE TO WRITE chronologically of my clients—many appeared on my horizon in the first years and remained with me to the end. Only lately, after an absence of five years, one of the faithful called and finding me still active although now retired, asked incredulously, "Why did you retire?" He could not understand how I could give up such a fascinating occupation. There were others, of course, who ordered only at long intervals, leaving me in doubt whether to continue to send them my catalogues. But for the most part I had a steady stream, if not a flood of buyers.

My early purchases had made it possible to issue catlogues with unusual books as well as the more familiar titles, and I learned that this combination attracted customers from many places in the United States and Canada. It was evident that the farther away they lived the more eagerly they sought my wares for, with the exception of a few ardent collectors, I remained unvisited by my own townsmen for some time.

It has been a pleasure touched with a feeling akin to homesickness to turn over the correspondence of my clientele. The wide variety of their collecting habits is amazing; their friendly and gracious letters warm my heart: their appreciation of any trouble I may have taken on their behalf makes me think my old friend was right: my business was a particularly rewarding one.

In the 1930's I had more doctors on my active mailing list than men of any other profession. When I remarked on this phenomenon to one of them, he said he was not surprised for as a student he had been encouraged to cultivate a hobby to relieve the strain of his professional life. I cannot quite agree with this explanation for it has been my experience that no amount of cultivation can turn a man into a book collector if the inborn spark is not present. As my business developed and the general way of life was violently affected by the war, the medical collectors either became fewer or were not so evident. I still, however, think with affection of such men as the late Dr. James Goodwin.

In the winter months I could always count on an interesting Wednesday afternoon with Dr. Goodwin as a companion, and I kept a corner for odds and ends with which to enliven his visit. Niagara Falls and Ontario were his pet fields of collecting. Both of these subjects led him down endless byways in his search for source material. His plan was to build up a reference library to show the development of Ontario from the first surveys to modern times. His collection of books, manuscripts and letters was linked with his rare stamps and his numerous prints of Canadian scenes. Even to the layman, early pictures and guide books of Niagara Falls are full of interest for do not the "Falls" belong to all of us? It arouses our speculation to discover that the island we now know by the abrupt and inapt name of Goat once was more appropriately and melodiously called Iris after the goddess of the rainbow. As early as 1800 a complete book was published on the subject of Niagara Falls by

John Maude who lived in America from 1793 to 1802 and wrote *A Visit to the Falls of Niagara in 1800* (London, 1826). There were eight engraved plates and three hundred copies issued, fifty of which were in royal 8vo, with proof plates. A collector's item, especially if a copy had "additional notes," sixteen pages tipped in after publication. Maude wrote this from pencilled notes made at the time of his visit. While this is rare it is not as scarce as many a small folder of later date and equal interest.

The monumental work by C. M. Dow called *Anthology and Bibliography of Niagara Falls,* 2 vols., Albany, 1921, gives some idea of the wealth of written material on this subject.

Dr. Goodwin's interest in it came naturally for he was born within the sound, not of Bow Bells, but of the "Many Waters" of the great falls.

Although he does not qualify as a medical man, I cannot refrain from mentioning the well-rounded collection on this subject gathered with so much intimate knowledge by Mr. Louis Blake Duff of Welland, Ontario.

"Osleriana" is, of course, a favourite subject of collecting for medical men throughout the world, and because of this there is not nearly enough available material to satisfy the demand. I was fortunate enough to be called in to sort out the vast collection of medical pamphlets accumulated by the late Dr. Jabez Elliott in a long and bookish life. When these found a resting-place on the shelves of numerous medical men they were, I know, greatly treasured. It is a pleasure to recall that from the beginning Dr. Elliott gave me encouragement.

Dr. E. P. Chagnon of Montreal was another of my faithful medical customers for many years and when I retired he wrote me a note of appreciation which I treasure. Canadian medical history, especially the rarer items, interested him. His other field was an unusual one for a private library—the collecting of complete runs of university and institutional periodicals, such as the *Queen's Quarterly* which goes back to 1893, the *Dalhousie Review, University of Toronto Quarterly,* and so on. These contain some of the best reading to be found in Canada, literary, philosophical and historical, but because their circulation has always been limited they are not widely known.

Only historically-minded members of the profession in all probability know of the existence of a very active group who have for many years published a quarterly known as *Historical Bulletin, Notes and Abstracts Dealing with Medical History,* issued by the Calgary Associate Clinic in conjunction with its Medico-Historical Meetings. This learned, though non-technical periodical is entertaining and definitely Canadian. In May, 1955, it reached its twentieth year, under the benign guidance of Dr. E. P. Scarlett, whose "notes from the common-place book of a medical reader" enlighten and beguile the reader in every issue. As the years went on many able writers in the Clinic and elsewhere took up their pens, and told the history of Canadian medical men and institutions in the pages of the *Bulletin.* A complete file of this paper, I predict, will be and perhaps is now a rare and valuable possession. Dr. Scarlett and the late Dr. Stanley of the Clinic were for many years stimulating customers.

I used to enjoy addressing letters to Dr. Shaw at Manitowaning, Ontario. Would that we had perpetuated more of these euphonious Indian names in our geography! Dr. Shaw was the medical man to the Indians in that part of Great Manitoulin Island, so graphically described by Anna Jameson in her *Winter Studies and Summer Rambles* (London, 1838). Here she saw the distribution of presents to 3,700 Indians, and attended the great council of chiefs. Dr. Shaw was deeply interested in the history of his patients and made a valuable collection of Indian language books. Many years after, when the doctor had laid down his stethoscope for the last time, these and other books came again into my possession. In my 39th catalogue (1949), under the heading "Aborigines," I noted "Many of the items are from the working library of a doctor who made a study of Indian dialects." They could not be described as "mint copies and unopened." Although they were neatly annotated and corrected, they were shabby and well thumbed, but needless to say were gathered up with avidity by collectors and librarians.

Dr. Shaw was not the only one of my medical customers who looked for books and pamphlets on Indian life in my catalogues. The most famous, though not by any means the most astute, was Fred Banting.

Fame came, as everyone knows, to Sir Frederick Banting at a very early age. With the perfecting of the discovery of insulin by him in association with Dr. C. H. Best, he emerged from the sheltered life of the laboratory into the turmoil of publicity. When I met him this phase, so overwhelming to one of his nature, had passed and he, through his new friends, the artists of the Group of Seven, had discovered another talent. He revelled in his ability to paint the wild scenery of Northern Ontario and Quebec and this led him to begin his collection of books on exploration. I believe he was happier then than at any time in his short life. Among the friends who influenced his taste was Miss Blodwen Davies. At that time, about the early 1930's, she had won a reputation as a writer on the Canadian scene and was engaged in the task of collecting material for a life of Tom Thomson, the artist who had lately met a tragic end in the northern woods. Many years after Miss Davies told me Banting had helped her in establishing her theory of how Thomson met his death.

Together these two interesting persons visited the Book Room. They generally came in the evening when they had plenty of time to examine the bookshelves. His taste for first editions of fur trader journals, such as Hearne, was expensive, but he wisely did not deny himself this extravagance. He had an ambition to study and perhaps later write a paper on Indian medicine and remedies. I doubt, however, that he ever got beyond the desire. Miss Davies' interest in artists and local history led her to other shelves and between these two brilliant personalities I was kept on my toes and enjoyed my evenings. Once Banting asked me to see his collection and to give him some advice as to how he should proceed. We spent an interesting hour in his studio-study-library, and alas, that was the last time we were to meet. With the breakup of his first marriage and his home life, he ceased to collect Canadiana. Had he lived through the war I feel sure he would have returned to the interests of this happy period of his life. Dr. Lloyd Stevenson, in his biography of Banting, refers to his visits to the Book Room. Thus is this small business immortalized.

In a brief autobiography called *Those Crowded Years, 1863-1944,* Dr. John Clarence Webster tells the story of his twofold life, first as a doctor and latterly as a collector of Canadiana. As the privately printed "life" in pamphlet form is little known to the public, I have jotted down some of the activities of this generous and able man.

Although many years of his active life were spent in Scotland and the United States, Webster was a true Maritimer, born and educated in New Brunswick. After graduating from Mount Allison he went to Edinburgh to study medicine and fell completely under the spell of his surroundings, so much so that had it not been for rigours of the climate and his health, he would probably have spent the rest of his life there. On his return to Canada as an obstetrician and gynecologist, he joined the staff at the Royal Victoria Hospital in Montreal. In 1899 he moved to Chicago and became a lecturer at Rush Medical College. From then on for twenty years he lived an extremely busy life as a medical man, only taking brief holidays for travel. In 1920, at the age of 48, he did what few men are able, or perhaps care to do, dropped the life for which he was trained, retired to his native province, regained his Canadian citizenship and became a student of Canadian history and an ardent book collector.

He seems to have plunged into the work with the same ardour as he had shown for his life as a doctor. It is flattering to my trade that he says, "I got in touch at once with the leading dealers," and in my records his name appears regularly for at least twenty years.

He identified historic sites and recorded his historical researches in fifty publications. He unveiled numerous cairns, including one in association with Dr. Lorne Pierce, to Bliss Carman at Fredericton. I can recall no other unofficial historian who devoted so much energy to his avocation.

His name is particularly linked with his collection of pictures of General Wolfe and his brochure, called *A Study of the Portraiture of James Wolfe,* is a unique account of the extraordinary number of portraits there are of this rather plain hero of Canadian history.

Dr. and Mrs. Webster worked together in the editing and translating of *Dierville: Port Royal* which was published as volume twenty of the Champlain Society, a monumental effort.

The Webster house at Shediac, N.B., was a meeting place for historians who came to see the books and pictures housed there and to engage in "good talk" with their hosts. This happy state of affairs continued until it became evident that disaster might come sometime to the collection in the absence of the owners. With the reorganization of the Provincial Museum at Fredericton, Dr. Webster generously donated his whole library to the province. This did not mean that he had ceased to collect. Almost weekly we received orders for old or new Canadian books and by return mail would come the remittance with some gracious words of appreciation. We knew that his health was failing and we dispatched the books with speed. His last letter came just three days before we read with regret the announcement of his death at the age of eighty-seven.

Not far away lived another medical man, a collector of great discrimination and knowledge, Dr. U. J. Bourjois of Tracadie, N.B. Strange to say, they did not know each other. Dr. Bourjois is descended from a long line of distinguished men and women of New France and Acadia. As few of us in other parts of Canada can number among our forebears so many historic Canadian names, I think it pertinent briefly to list a few of them. Only a genealogist, however, could do justice to the Bourjois family tree. Most of these early arrivals on our shores seem to have been forthright persons, who took a leading part in settlement and discoveries as well as in wars.

On Dr. Bourjois' maternal side was René Gaultière de Varennes, a noble of France, who came to New France as a lieutenant in the famous Régiment de Carignan-Salières. The Regiment was disbanded and all the officers became Seigneurs of New France in 1666, René's title being Seigneur de Varennes. He married a daughter of Pierre de Boucher, a seigneur, and for thirty years Governor of Three Rivers under the King of France. From this union came the famous explorers known as discoverers of the West, under the name of La Vérendrye, whose exploits are published in Volume IX of the Champlain Society publications.

The Bourjois came to Acadia in 1642, and there founded the Bourjois settlement of traders in the Isthmus of Chignecto, which became the seigneury of Lavalière, the last capital of Acadie where forts were lost to the British. There is a monument near Fort Beauséjour to the memory of Jacques Bourjois, junior. The doctor can even boast some Scottish blood in his veins through Pierre Melauson (his real name was MacLaughlin) who came to Acadia with Sir William Alexander's Scottish settlers. Many of these returned but Melauson stayed and threw in his lot with the Acadians. In one of my letters from Dr. Bourjois he ends appropriately: "Vive le Canada! Vive l'Angleterre! Vive la France! Vive l'Ecossi!"

The rest of my customers I am unable to fit so neatly into professional groups. To be sure I had bankers, engineers, miners, industrial presidents and workers, school teachers, explorers and postmen; I even had a lighthouse-keeper, an historically-minded man who spent his time off duty aloft searching country churchyards in an effort to complete a list of early settlers in his county. I have selected a few—some whose names are famous, although that did not necessarily make them more interesting as collectors, others because their knowledge of Canadian books was wide and deep, and again others whose requests came from places remote from Canada.

It has been affirmed that the Canadian writers whose names are best known beyond our shores are Service, de la Roche and Leacock—a mixed bag. I can at least claim the latter as a constant client.

At first I used to flatter myself that Stephen Leacock examined my catalogues item by item. Later I wondered whether there wasn't a compelling attraction about the letter "L". Be that as it may, he did not overlook entry

No. 242 in catalogue 15 (1935) which read: "Leacock, S., editor. *Lahontan's Voyages,* with Notes and Introduction by Stephen Leacock. Graphic Publishers. Ott. 1931. Scarce."

A special delivery letter arrived from Montreal beginning, as usual: Messrs. Dora Hood's Book Room, Dear Sirs:—Send immediately No. 242—I never saw a copy of this book, nor was I ever paid for the work I did in editing. Yours truly, Stephen Leacock.

This threw an interesting sidelight on a courageous if short-lived venture in publishing the works of Canadian authors. All I knew at the time was that a quantity of books bearing the name Graphic Publishers, Ottawa, on their title pages had a few years before appeared on the bargain counters of departmental stores in Montreal and Toronto and that we, the dealers, had bought all we could lay our hands on. Among them were a few copies of Leacock's *Lahontan.* It was obvious that the concern had failed and we were to reap the only rewards. There were other seductive titles which later became collector's items and the stories behind these I shall relate elsewhere. For years the Graphic Publishers' titles drifted in and out of my stock and though I asked, no one seemed to know who had been responsible for the venture. With the pressure of business a thing of the past I began to search. The Toronto Reference Library had no record, not even a catalogue of the Graphic books. This was strange in that otherwise fount of information. Then it was suggested to me that I write to Madge MacBeth, a veteran in the field of Canadian authorship. From the remote Canary Islands came the answer. The Graphic Publishers, she wrote, owed its existence to a printer named Henry Miller. With no previous experience in the precarious business of publishing anything, he had tackled the most hazardous of all gambles, that of producing Canadian books. That was in 1924. *The Land of Afternoon*, by Gilbert Knox (Madge MacBeth), was his first title, a satire on Ottawa society; it made quite a stir in the capital and proved to be his most profitable book.

Lack of advertising was responsible for the failure of the firm which came in 1932, in spite of the many attractive titles issued. It was evident to me that someone with taste and discrimination had advised Miller in his choice of authors. I suspected it was the late Lawrence Burpee. His vast knowledge and kindness of heart fitted into the picture very neatly.

But I must now return to Leacock. It was an amusing episode in the day's work to produce for an author his brain child, unrecorded and evidently forgotten. Lately I found an interesting sequel to this story. In 1954 Dr. Gerhard R. Lomer, former librarian of McGill, published a book: *Stephen Leacock, a Check-list and Index of his Writings*. True to my instinct to search bibliographies, I looked up the entry headed *Lahontan's Voyages* and read:

> The Friedman copy in the Redpath Library, McGill University, contains the following holograph note by Leacock: "I received, through Dr. Burpee of Ottawa, a contract with the Graphic Company to do an introduction to Lahontan's Journal, with notes . . . The Company failed and paid nothing . . . But I found out long afterwards that some copies of the book had gone through the press, though it was never on the market . . . I was never able to get a copy . . ."

This, of course, was written before my copy reached Leacock, and he probably had forgotten he had written the note. The statement about Lawrence Burpee confirmed my suspicion that Miller relied on his help for the choice of the historical works issued by Graphic.

In my file of the year 1943 I find a sheaf of letters from

Leacock, mostly written from Old Brewery Bay, Orillia, Ontario. He was evidently anxious to study the works of his fellow wits for he asked me to supply him with certain books by A. P. Herbert, Robert Benchley, Harry Graham, Ring Lardner, John Kendrick and Max Adler. Was he at this late date considering a change in his own brand of humour? In another letter he says he is sending me "an abstract of what I am writing, 10,000 words under the title 'Canada and the Sea'," and asks me to send a list of helpful books. I am sure this abstract never reached me for I would have treasured it. I seem however, to have sent him a good collection of books on the Maritimes. The Lomer check list reveals that *Canada and the Sea* was published in Montreal by Alvah M. Beatty in December, 1944. I have never seen a copy of this posthumously published work.

One other interesting sidelight appears in the preface of this bibliography. Dr. Lomer says a special effort was made to examine the first edition of each of Leacock's works. Fortunately, one of his old pupils, Mr. Norman H. Friedman (an intermittent customer of mine) had made a collection of Leacock first editions and Leacockiana, which he later turned over to the Library of McGill.

I am sorry to say Leacock never came to my office but continued to correspond with me on the subject of Canadian books. At last I decided to break through the business-like impersonality of our correspondence and tell him that as a small girl named Dora Ridout, I remembered seeing him when he was a young man toiling at his hated tasks as a school master at Upper Canada College. I was the bosom friend of the daughter of another master, the stern and unapproachable "Stony" Jackson. Mrs. Jarley's wax works were produced yearly at the College, much as the operas of Gilbert and Sullivan are today, and

Leacock performed the part of Mrs. Jarley with gusto. This revelation opened the flood gates of memory and produced the following letter:

April 3rd, 1953.

Dear Mrs. Hood:

I had no idea you were a Ridout, having much lost track of Toronto. I think I taught your older brother at the old college on King St. and remember your older sister (or aunt)[1] of about Pelham's (Edgar) age. I went with her out driving once, that is with Pelham and his fiancée soon-to-be on the front seat. I sat with Miss Ridout on the back seat (and had the best place). I recall several little girls (dimly) who used to be companions of Isabel Jackson, no doubt you were one; but you are mistaken in putting Peacock[2] and Collinson there together. Colly left before Peacock came.

Yours,

Stephen Leacock.

Later he sent me a copy of a privately printed brochure called *My old college, 1843-1943,* an appeal for funds for McGill and written in his most diverting style. Then came his last book *Happy Stories—Just to Make You Smile.* This he inscribed to me with the comment, "It is about the Toronto you just don't remember."

Dr. Lomer's lengthy bibliography of Leacock's books and pamphlets shows how industrious he was, and although his books were issued in large editions and sold well, it is not an easy task to assemble a complete set. Many were published only in the United States and perhaps did not sell widely in Canada. I remember a young parish priest asking me to supply him with all the titles I could get. I could not help feeling that Leacock would have enjoyed the thought of the sterner studies being laid aside while the priest dipped into *Nonsense Novels.*

[1]He has mixed relationships.
[2] Sir Edward Peacock.

Australians are said to be especially fond of our Leacock. We need not be ashamed of this choice, even if his humour is apt to run in a groove. We can absorb a great deal more of this commodity than we are offered in the world today. But I was to discover other interests in Canada by a small group of highly intelligent Australians and for some years experienced in imagination the warm clasp of hands across the sea.

Via the far Pacific Ocean my earliest catalogues found their way to the Mitchell Library in Sydney, Australia. It was there that they fell into the hands of four ardent collectors and through these I made two staunch friends and one enemy.

Australians, and particularly those of New South Wales, are fortunate to have fallen heir, at a comparatively early date, to a rich collection of books, manuscripts and pictures relating to their country by the will of David Scott Mitchell. I knew when I dispatched my catalogues that the Mitchell Library was considered one of the great libraries of the world, and sometimes wondered how it came to pass that such a young country possessed a collection of books ranking with the best. After my retirement I had time to satisfy my curiosity and this led me to read a book written by Margaret Burton called *Famous Libraries.* In this I learned something about David Mitchell, though not nearly enough. He was born in 1836, an Australian of Scottish descent. Antiquarian booksellers everywhere must have known him as a collector, for by 1898 he had amassed a collection of 61,000 pieces of Australiana of the greatest value. Among the treasures bequeathed to his country were samples of the earliest printing in Australia, narratives in manuscripts and books of the navigators and inland explorers, diaries and books of clergymen, missionaries, doctors and governors and, as we shall recount, the records left by members of the Penal Colony. To comply with the terms of the will the country had to provide a building. This was completed in 1910, three years after Mitchell's death, and since that time more than 70,000 books have been acquired.

When *Famous Libraries* was published in 1937, there was no printed catalogue of the Mitchell collection and those who wished to consult the card catalogue and to use the library had to have accredited cards of admission. My four collectors were evidently among this privileged number, for with the arrival of my first catalogue letters came to me from all of them. This was very encouraging, except that they all wanted the same scarce books. To Canadians, these are known as narratives of the political exiles of the Rebellion of 1837-1838 in Australia and Van Diemen's Land.

It was easy to see that my correspondents were deeply interested in the history of their country and fanatical bibliophiles, and I knew trying to satisfy them all would be fraught with difficulties. Dr. George Mackaness, O.B.E., M.A., etc., of Sydney, N.S.W., and Dr. W. E. H. Crowther of Hobart Town, Tasmania, from the first wrote me friendly and gracious letters and I have no compunction in confessing that on occasions I favoured them. My other correspondent was Mr. Justice J. A. Ferguson, the learned compiler of several volumes of the monumental bibliography of Australiana.

Students of the Rebellion of 1837-1838 have deplored the sentence of exile meted out to a number of the rebels at the end of hostilities. It is reported that Durham wished to avoid the death sentence and had the pleasant island of Bermuda in mind as the place of exile. To only a few, however, fell this lot, the remainder, 140 in all, were destined to undergo the horrors of the exile ship's journey of nearly six months to Tasmania and New South Wales.

They were a mixed company on the ship *Buffalo,* eighty-two from Upper Canada and fifty-eight from Lower Canada, and among this number were a few Americans, mostly of Fenian tendency, who had joined the fight. When the wretched boatload arrived at Hobart the prisoners from Upper Canada debarked while the rest went on to New South Wales. There is no doubt about the misery of their lives during the eight long years of their exile, for nine of them recorded it in books issued after their return. These narratives have always aroused a certain interest in Canada, but to the Australians they are of tremendous importance. Printed reports of the life of political prisoners at that period are scarce, for few had the powers to describe their lives let alone the means to appear in print. It is, therefore, quite remarkable that even nine of the 140 have given us more or less accurate accounts.

A list of these books is given with the hope, though perhaps a vain one, that some reader may come across copies. My estimate of their rarity is also given based on my own experience. Those published in the United States are:

Gates, W: *Recollections of Life in Van Diemen's Land.* New York: Lockport, 1850. Scarce.

Marsh, R: *Seven Years of My Life or Narrative of a Patriot Exile, etc.* Buffalo: 1847. This is the rarest.

Miller, L. W: *Notes of an Exile to Van Diemen's Land.* Fredonia, 1848. I had this twice only.

Snow, S: *The Exiles Return, etc.* Cleveland: 1846. Scarce.

Waite, B: *Letters from Van Diemen's Land, etc.* Buffalo: 1843. This is the most often found. It was published by Waite's wife while he was still absent.

Wright, S: *Narrative and Recollections of Van Diemen's Land, etc by Caleb Lyon.* New York: Lyonsdale, 1844. Scarce.

Heustis, D. D.: *A Narrative of the Adventures and Sufferings of Capt. David Heustis in Van Diemen's Land during his Long Captivity.* Boston: 1847. Very scarce.

Since writing this account of the "Exile" books, it is exciting to be able to record that a copy of the rarest of all, *Marsh,* has turned up lately in the Book Room. under the new régime. In an article on this subject in volume 9 of the Ontario Historical Society Dr. J. D. Barnett says: "I have seen only one copy of *Marsh,* the personal copy of Dr. F. H. Severence of Buffalo." This new find has gone to make more complete the very extensive holdings on the Rebellion of 1837-8 in the library of the University of Western Ontario. The acquisition of this rare volume by the library was particularly appropriate as Dr. Barnett, who made a close study of the "Exile" narratives, gave his library of forty thousand books to Western University Library and, indeed, laid the foundation of its collections.

Those published in Montreal and written in French are:

Ducharme, L: *Journal d'un exile politique, aux terres Australes.* Montreal: 1845. Now scarce. Only three copies known in Australia.

Prier, F. X: *Notes d'un condamné politique de 1838.* Montreal: 1864 and 2nd ed. 1884. Now scarce.

It is about these two French accounts that I have a story to tell. But first I must explain what happened when my four collectors all wanted the same books.

I was anxious, of course, to satisfy these faraway clients and to work up a larger connection in Australia if possible. All of their wants were duly recorded on my cards but, of course, they all wanted the rarer *Exiles.* As so often happens in the book business, soon one of the wanted books mysteriously turned up. It was "Miller" and I had to choose between them. I wrote offering it to Justice Ferguson who promptly cabled for it and probably spread the glad news among the others that he had at last secured a copy. At that the most touchy of the group wrote in no uncertain terms that I had overlooked his request which he felt I had had before the others and to put it mildly he was very much annoyed. I was devoutly thankful that "mountains and a waste of seas" divided us. Alas! I was never able to atone for my crime by sending another copy. The other two proved themselves to be collectors of the nobler breed and took it in good part.

Fortunately, I was able to be of real service to one of those I had disappointed, and the other, Dr. Crowther of Hobart Town, remained a delightful pen friend for the rest of my career.

George Mackaness was an historian of note in Australia and up to 1949 devoted his talents to producing eighteen privately printed Australian historical monographs. He had a flair for unearthing manuscripts and rare printed material bearing on the early history of his country. One brochure, for instance, dealt with R.L.S. and his associations with Australia, while another gave Captain Bligh's discoveries and observations on Van Diemen's Land.

In 1943 Dr. Mackaness wrote to say he had decided to bring out as his ninth historical monograph a translation of Leon Ducharme's *Journal d'un exile politique aux terres Australes,* which he had purchased from me. In order to be well versed in the Canadian Rebellion he wished me to send him all the books I considered pertinent. This I knew would include some scarce books and as the Japanese fleet was still in command of the Pacific Ocean I hesitated to send them, but as my client too knew the risk we ran I decided finally to proceed with the order. I am happy to relate that the whole shipment arrived in good order to the delight of my friend. Among the books I selected were:

Lord Durham's *Report on the Affairs of British North America.* I was able to get the complete report in reprint.

Decelles, A. D.: *The Patriots of '37.* 1916.

Head, Sir F. Bond: *Narrative.* London: 1839.

Lindsay's *Life and Times of William Lyon Mackenzie.* 2 vols. 1862.

Read, D. B.: *The Rebellion of 1837.* Toronto: 1896.

Guillet, E. C.: *The Lives and Times of the Patriots.* Toronto: 1938. This proved a source of much information for the purpose.

David, L. O.: *Les Patriotes de 1837-38.* Montreal: 1884.

Report of the State Trials . . . held at Montreal in 1838-1839 . . . exhibiting a complete history of the late Rebellion in Lower Canada. Montreal: 1839. 2 vols. Dr. Mackaness had written to say he had discovered in the Mitchell Library the warrants for the prisoners and this book was, therefore, intensely interesting to him.

Theller, E. A.: *Canada in 1837-38,* showing, by historical facts, the causes of the late attempted revolution and of its failure . . . together with the personal adventures of the author and others, etc. 2 vols. Phila.: 1841. Theller called himself a Brig.-General in the Rebellion. He was captured and imprisoned in Quebec and had he not escaped would have shared the fate of the luckless exiles.

In spite of the War in the Pacific many letters passed between Dr. Mackaness and myself. It was a strange experience to assist an author at such a distance and I did what I could. For instance, he wanted if possible to trace the descendants of those who returned to Quebec, but aside from Ducharme and Prier, who had some education, the rest had sunk back into the masses from which they came. Of the fifty-eight sent to New South Wales, two died, fifty-five ultimately returned to Canada and only one, Joseph Mareau, remained in Australia. He married and settled in the west coast. Although a hundred years had passed since the episode, Mr. Mackaness, after persistent search, at last found the son of the original Mareau.

In 1944 a letter arrived with the announcement that the monograph was finished and one of the ten presentation copies was on its way here. There was quite a flutter in the Book Room when it appeared that the book had been dedicated to me! I was flattered, of course, and took it not only as a tribute to myself but to all book dealers whose work so often goes unacknowledged. The preface gave a brief history of the political troubles in the Canadas and I was eager to see what conclusion the author had come to. Knowing little of the controversy which has ever since divided Canadian historians, it appeared he had taken a strong slant in favour of the Government Party. I asked Dr. Mackaness to let me buy as many as he could spare of the ninety copies for sale and they went "like hot cakes."

As his eighteenth monograph he produced in 1949 his excellent translation of Prier's *Notes d'un condamné politique de 1838.* Both Ducharme and Prier wrote well and with great sincerity and probably gave a truer picture of life in Australia than the other more bitter accounts. After many weary months of penal servitude they became ticket-of-leave men and were free to find their own employment. This was a tribute to their characters and relieved the monotony of their existence. Nevertheless, the appalling sense of separation from their native land weighed unbearably upon them.

Prier writes:

Nothing on earth, I am sincerely of the opinion, could have persuaded us to remain far away from our own native land, neither wealth nor distinctions. We were a-hungered and a-thirst for our homeland, we were consumed with a desire to return to Canada, to see again our families, our friends, our beautiful countryside, to salute the belfries of our parishes, to speak French, and to gaze on the sight of our good Canadian-French customs.

How did they return? The mills of justice ground exceeding slow, but at last a general pardon was affected and through the sacrifice of their kin and friends and the good offices in London of John Arthur Roebuck they at length made the long journey home.

Copies of these two translations may be seen in most of the leading libraries in Eastern Canada and are well worth reading.

There are two other historical links between Canada and Australia at about the same period as the Exiles though only remotely connected. Sir George Arthur became Lieut.-Governor of Van Diemen's Land in 1823 and in 1838 held the same office in Upper Canada where he remained until the union of the two provinces in 1841. In 1950 the Arthur papers on Upper Canada were purchased from his descendants by the Toronto Public Library and already four volumes of them have been published with more to come.

Sir John Franklin, whom Canadians are apt to consider as one of their most notable personalities, spent the years between 1836 and 1843 as Lieut.-Governor of Van Diemen's Land. It is evident that the frozen regions of our Arctic appealed more to his adventurous spirit than did the tropical beauty of the southern island for he returned to the scenes of his first two Arctic expeditions to embark on his fateful third voyage.

I have said nothing about my correspondence with Dr. W. E. L. Crowther which continued so pleasantly for many years. All our book transactions must have been accomplished with satisfaction on both sides, for I remember little of them. In our letters we frequently wandered far from the subject of the Exiles and I became deeply interested in his writings on the historical background of his remote and beautiful island. One of his pamphlets lies before me now and I cannot resist the temptation to tell briefly the story of an enterprising ancestor of his.

There were a succession of doctors bearing his name in Tasmania, beginning with a naval surgeon who settled there upon release from service. The most colourful of them, according to my friend, was his grandfather who became the Hon. W. L. Crowther, F.R.C.S., C.M.Z.S.

As a young boy in Van Diemen's Land he was a keen naturalist and collector, the wild life of the island giving him ample scope for his taste and skill. He was apprenticed to his father, a surgeon, but to qualify as a doctor it was necessary for him to make the long and expensive journey to London and the Continent. He decided not to ask his father for financial aid but to take his specimens of Tasmanian fauna, alive and dead, to England and there to dispose of them for cash. It was a difficult and hazardous undertaking which he recounted in lively entries in his diary. In February, 1839, he boarded on the barque *Emu,* accompanied by cages, crates and tanks containing fishes, parrots, wombats, "devils" and wallabys and numerous other livestock besides trunks of cured skins and pelts.

The voyage was long and frequently tempestuous and unrelieved by a landfall. They rounded the Horn and steered northeast through pirate-infested waters and all the way the livestock had to be fed and kept clean and healthy. Albatrosses were shot and fishes caught to eke out the food supply he had brought with him. Near the end of the voyage he inspected, with some misgivings, the boxes of skins and rejoiced to find all 493 of them in good order. He confessed he was heartily sick of the work, but not sorry he had undertaken it.

On arrival in England he was able to sell his whole collection to the Zoological Society, probably (so says his grandson) through the generosity of the Earl of Derby. The amount was £300 which allowed him to complete his course at St. Thomas' Hospital and to proceed to graduate work in Paris and Brussels. He returned home as surgeon on a ship and on his arrival was made a member of Sir John Franklin's small Tasmanian Naturalists Society.

For many years he sent specimens to Sir William Fowler at the Museum of the Royal College of Surgeons, among them thirty complete skeletons of whales, captured by his own whalers from his own ships. Surely he must be the only doctor on record who, besides conducting a medical practice, owned and operated a fleet of whalers.

My clients "down under" increased in number until the fateful hour when the "sterling area" came into being. From then on difficulty in securing permits brought to an end this interesting Commonwealth exchange.

As a people we have been slow to study our past, especially our heritage from the aborigines.

"They are dead," wrote an unknown hand, "their cause is lost, their enemy has written their history."

On my shelves were many of these histories, together with archaelogical revelations of the Indians' dim past. I had an unfeigned regard for these books.

Among the rarer Canadian books on the Indians is Paul Kane's *Wandering of an Artist among the Indians of North America* (London, 1859). There are thirteen illustrations, and eight coloured plates and a folding map. The title chosen by Kane, or perhaps suggested by his publishers was truly an inspiration, and it was through the sale of my first copy of this unique book that I began my long and enlightening association with David I. Bushnell, Jr., of Washington, D.C. The price, I remember, was $60 and the value has risen steadily as copies become scarcer and the demand increases. Mr. Bushnell was a man of scholarly tastes and had led an active life in pursuit of his studies, untrammelled by any need to add to his income. In his early days he had toured Europe to make notes of the collections of relics of the North American Indian in the continental museums. Later he travelled far and wide in his own country engaged in scientific archaeology. The bibliography of his writings on his research runs into many pages. But his most valuable contribution on our aborigines, because it is almost unique, is his collection of sketches from life by the early artists of the activities of the North American Indian tribes.

It was after his study of the *Wanderings* that Mr. Bushnell wrote to ask me if I could possibly get him a sketch, not a studio-finished picture, by Paul Kane. I replied that I was not in any sense a picture dealer but that I had always been interested in early Canadian pictures, having a few of my own, and would do what I could, although I held out no high hopes of success. Then it occurred to me that years ago I had spent a delightful afternoon with Mrs. Allan Cassels when she had actually shown me two books of Paul Kane's sketches. She was the daughter of the Hon. George W. Allan who had, on Kane's return from his wanderings, commissioned him to do a series of a hundred pictures from his sketches. The paintings remained in the Allan family for years until they were finally acquired by E. B. Osler (afterwards Sir Edmund) and presented by him to the Royal Ontario Museum where they now hang and greatly enhance the archaeological galleries.

With some misgivings I went again to see Mrs. Cassels in her charming Victorian house in Wellesley Place. Between the cabinets of exquisite Chelsea china the walls were thickly covered with pictures and photographs and on the tables books added that "sweet serenity" which bespoke the owner's tastes.

I told her at once that I had come to ask her to sell a Paul Kane sketch to Mr. Bushnell, giving her a thumbnail picture of his career. It speaks well for her understanding for though reluctant to "sell her birthright for a mess of pottage," as she put it, she consented to let him have a small picture of an Ojibway camp on one of the Spider islands of Lake Huron.

It was quite a triumph for me, and shortly after Mr. Bushnell announced that he and his mother would like to spend the summer in Toronto and would I recommend a suitable place to stay. His mother had become blind and his tender devotion to her was extremely touching. She, on her part, took great delight in telling me that she was only seventeen years older than her son.

I confess, while I looked forward to meeting this unusual couple, I was a little overwhelmed at the prospect of being responsible for their enjoyment of Canada. I had hoped to receive Mr. Bushnell attractively clad in a summer frock, and still vividly remember my dismay when he arrived at nine in the morning while I was shaking the Book Room duster on my doorstep clad in a brief and workaday morning smock. I could only hope that he found me picturesque, while I soon fell under his charm.

We made plans to visit some of the older artists with the hope that they might be induced to part with examples of their sketches of Indian life.

Next day we went by appointment to call on Mr. George Reid, at that time well up in his eighties, but still working in his spacious studio in Wychwood Park. Mrs. Reid, as Gertrude Spurr, had made a name for herself as an artist, and the house reflected her love of blended colours and comfort. It was June and I was proud to show my visitor the woodland beauty of the park. The two men were soon deep in conversation and before we left Mr. Reid had parted with some of his interesting early sketches.

Our next call was upon an even more venerable artist, Mr. Mower Martin. When twenty-one years of age Mr. Martin had come to Canada in 1859 in search of health and first settled for a time in Muskoka, near Bracebridge. He was highly successful in his choice of a health resort for when we visited him he was in his ninety-second year. His vast studio was still lined with enormous canvases, some half-finished. But his interest in pictorial art seemed to have languished and he was now devoting himself to music. He sat in one corner of the study with a violin tucked under his chin while eight others hung on the wall beside him. He explained to us that he was still undecided as to which of the nine had the best tone and then turned to scrape out a squeaky tune on another.

But his daughter Miss Martin was helpful and took us into another room where she had assembled a number of highly interesting old sketch books. She explained that her father had spent much of his life travelling about Canada, the west coast Indian life especially appealing to his sense of form in their boats and totem poles.

Mr. Bushnell was in his element and selected a number of sketches he hoped to be allowed to purchase. But Miss Martin insisted that her father must be consulted, although he had long since forgotten about them. Seeing his old sketches aroused the artist in him. He flatly refused to consider parting with them. "They are my stock in trade," he declared. "I might very well want to use them, sometime." In the end, however, he gave his consent, and we left him still poring over the work of his faraway youth.

Mr. Bushnell was pleased when later I was able to get him a copy of a charming and now little known book illustrated by Mower Martin in 1907. The title read: *Canada. Painted by T. Mower Martin, R.C.A. Described by Wilfred Campbell, LL.D.* Published by A. Black. London, 1907.

There are seventy-seven coloured plates of Canadian scenes from the Maritimes to the Pacific, and they are delightful. A book such as this is badly needed now when educated people are settling here from all over the world. I have had my share of these people come to me for something more than postcards to send home to their friends and relations. I know of only this and one other book which strangely enough was published in Germany in 1926. It is called *Canada,* and the compiler was Louis Hamilton who also wrote the introduction. There are 288 excellent photogravures, the titles being in four languages, a point well worth noting for future issues of such books.

After our call on Mr. Martin, I produced my trump card, an appointment to introduce Mr. Bushnell to Mrs. Allan Cassels. I had no anxiety about this meeting. They were people of much the same tastes and I felt I was bestowing a benefit on them both in bringing them together. To arrange such meetings is one of the keenest satisfactions in the life of a bookman.

I was due to leave town shortly on my yearly holiday with my children. Mr. Bushnell, I knew, would find much to interest him in our Museum, Art Gallery and picture shops, until my return in a few weeks.

The friendship with Mrs. Cassels resulted in the

publication of the most valuable brochure on Paul Kane which has appeared so far. Around a number of sketches from Kane's note book Mr. Bushnell wrote a pamphlet for the Smithsonian Institute called *Sketches of Paul Kane in the Indian Country, 1845-1848* (Smith. Misc. Coll. No. 99). In the preface are many sidelights on Kane's career gathered from Mrs. Cassels' reminiscences of talks with her father. Kane had an unfortunate habit through carelessness or fatigue of neglecting to add date and place to many of his sketches, but Mr. Bushnell's researches helped to supply this need. The portrait in this pamphlet is a hitherto unpublished one of the artist. On the death of Mrs. Cassels the priceless sketch books were stored in the vaults of a trust company awaiting their final disposition by her grandson. They are now in the safekeeping of the Royal Ontario Museum. To my mind these sketches are infinitely finer than the finished pictures. It is to be hoped that some day funds will be forthcoming to publish them.

By the time I had returned to town Mr. Bushnell had accumulated at least two Verners and several Armstrongs to add to his collection. William Armstrong's work as an artist depicting Canadian scenes is not widely known and yet in numerous water-colour pictures he recorded with great accuracy and skill the rural, urban and wild life of Ontario. Mr. Armstrong as a young man came to Canada in 1851 and took employment as an engineer on the Grand Trunk Railway. In 1870 he went west with the expedition under General Wolseley to quell Riel's first insurrection and returned with many sketches of this adventure. Later as a surveyor his work took him to the Great Lakes region and with his professional paraphernalia went his sketch block, pencils and paints. His companions were chiefly Indian guides and his means of transport birchbark canoes. When the day's work was over he sketched the scenes around during the long bright evenings of early summer. This faculty of putting on paper the activities of his guides, their manner of handling the immense canoes, the never-ceasing employment of the squaws and the bold scenery of the shores they followed, must have been close to his heart. When winter came and he was once more in his snug house known as the "Priory" on Augusta Avenue in Toronto, he put the finishing touches to his work. Being a methodical man he signed and dated every picture. I was fortunate once in finding a picture of his showing the village life of a group of Indians camping beside the Sault Ste. Marie. I never saw a picture of Indian life so full of animated detail. In the background could be seen the steamers passing through the canal. Gone forever are such subjects.

Mr. Bushnell was fascinated by Armstrong's work and was astonished that he was so little known in this country. For accuracy in recording the shape of canoes, wigwams and Indian costume, Armstrong far exceeded Paul Kane. This was Mr. Bushnell's expert opinion.

Water-colours of the Victorian age are now relegated to the attic or entirely discarded. We would do well, however, not to overlook an Armstrong when it comes our way. Even the John Ross Robertson collection possesses only a single picture, of his, the departure of troops to the west in 1870 at the railway station at Toronto.

In 1940 I passed through Washington on the way to South Carolina and had the pleasure of once more meeting Mr. Bushnell. On this occasion he showed me through the Smithsonian Institute, where I saw the original pictures of Catlin hung somewhat ignominiously along a crowded corridor of an upper floor.

I was asked by my distinguished guide what I would like to see in the vast overcrowded building. For a moment I was fairly cornered and then a bright idea came and I said, "I would like to see a model of the Peking Man skull, found by a Canadian, Dr. Davidson Black in 1929." I was shown a copy, the workmanship so perfect that it might have been mistaken at first glance for the original. Now the models are all that remain to us, the original vanished during the invasion of China by the Japanese.

It was a great treat to be shown Mr. Bushnell's complete collection of Indian pictures. Many of the artists' names I knew, through my art books, such as Eastman, Webber, and White who was the first English artist to visit America in 1585.

I heard in 1941 with great regret that Mr. Bushnell had died and it was some time before I was able to discover what had become of his picture collection. It is now in the Peabody Museum at Harvard, and well worth a visit.

Buying books from catalogues is a very old custom among collectors and it is surprising what a satisfactory way most of them find it. There are others, and I confess I am one of them, who like to walk into a bookshop and see what they are buying. Again, auction buying to a goodly number is the only way, for after carefully calculating their bids, the would-be buyers relish the excitement of waiting for the results.

Such a one was the late Mr. W. P. Whitton of Hamilton, Ontario. He had a remarkably select and almost perfect library in the field he had chosen. His books represented the first published accounts of the early period of Canadian history. For instance, his aim was to possess as complete a set as could be found of the original Jesuit *Relations.* These accounts sent back to France by the Jesuit missionaries of New France were a curious mixture of religious dissertations and narratives of their encounters with the Indians, the fur traders and the French settlers. I was under the impression, gleaned, I think, from Mr. Whitton's conversation that the most complete collection of these source books was in the John Carter Brown library of Providence, R.I. But lately, to bring myself up to date, I wrote to Mr. Lawrence C. Worth, the keeper of the Brown collection and an authority on this subject. In his reply of January, 1957, he generously disclaimed any superiority. "I am not by any means sure," he says, "that our collection of Jesuit *Relations* can be described as the most complete in existence. I am inclined to think that the Lenox collection in New York Public Library is larger than ours. I think furthermore that the Harvard collection is very good indeed and the private collections of Mr. James Bell of Minneapolis and Mr. Robert Dechert of Gulph Mills, Penna., are of extraordinary completeness."

In the course of time Mr. Whitton was not far behind. It was my good fortune to add another to his collection. With the Neilson library I had acquired a perfect copy of Père Jerome Lalemant's *Relation,* 1663, bound in the original vellum with the signature of the Hon. John Neilson on the fly leaf. This was not the martyred Lalemant of Fort Marie, but he who so vividly described the earthquake near Quebec which gave the name to Mont Tremblant. I offered this to Mr. Whitton at $225 and he ordered it by return mail with the request that I deliver it by hand and allow him to show me his collection.

Some people are starved for want of books. Mr. Whitton was hungry for book talk and I was a ready listener. Never have I seen a library in such perfect condition. I think without exception all his books were in "mint" condition, either in their original bindings or handsomely leather bound and tooled. Huge ledgers, also heavily bound in leather, recorded all his purchases, with name of book, where bought, date, price, and other details, such as former owner if famous in any way. Another ledger recorded his "desiderata" with recorded prices from catalogues and auction records. Perhaps it was all just a little too perfect and showed a pride of possession that detracted from, rather than added to, the appeal of such a library. But I must be fair to Mr. Whitton. Book-collecting was not a hobby to him. It was his whole life. He told me regretfully that he knew only one or two people who had the least appreciation of the extent and value of his books. After his death it was some time before the executors decided how to dispose of the books. Finally a list was circulated and bids asked for. With few exceptions the collection went to the Montreal Civic Library, although most of us in the trade put in bids.

Mr. Whitton's propensity for buying by auction and his penchant for early Jesuit material reminds me of my interesting experience at a New York sale.

Book auctions have not been notable successes in Canada, at least not in my memory. In a country such as ours, where collectors are thinly spread over a vast area, only in Montreal and Toronto would any auctioneer venture to hold an auction entirely devoted to books.

The great centres of London, Paris and New York will continue to be the principal auction marts for many years to come and the yearly volumes of Book Prices Current and its British equivalent Book-auction Records the source of price information. Relatively few Canadian books come up for auction even in these centres and it is noticeable that prices vary a good deal from year to year.

Early in the 1930's, although the peak of high prices

had passed, the New York firm known then by the cumbersome title of "American Art Galleries, Anderson Galleries," announced a sale of purely Canadian books. This firm, which was on a par with Sotheby and Christie of London, had long been considered the fashionable place to consign one's books when it became desirable to part with them. The library to be sold on this occasion belonged to one of the most famous book collectors in Canada, Victor Morin. His is a name to conjure with in all matters pertaining to the written history of Canada. Not only is he the author of many books and pamphlets but his name has for years headed the list of patrons in innumerable historical societies, libraries and authors' associations. As the owner of a vast collection of Canadiana, he probably ranks the most notable, so far, in the annals of Canadian collectors.

Mr. Morin was at the period of his New York auction about seventy years of age. Among the rare items he offered for sale were some outstanding Jesuit manuscripts which he felt would draw more bidders in New York than in the limited Canadian market.

I decided to attend this sale as much for the experience as for anything I might be able to buy. In New York there were a number of firms with which I had done business and it would be to my advantage to call on them. Both of these experiences, I felt, would enlarge my horizon.

I confess I was nervous when I went, as it was the custom, a day or two before the sale, to inspect the books in the imposing building on 58th Street occupied by the Art Galleries. The deep crimson carpet, the uniformed lackeys who unlocked the handsome bookcases at our request, and solemnly placed the books before us on long polished tables, the detached silence of the other dealers and collectors as they pored over the volumes, and the general air of great wealth increased my timidity. I wondered vaguely how far my limited roll of Canadian dollars would go when the bidding started. It was a relief then to be greeted by my good friend Georges Ducharme from Montreal. He seemed to sense my forlorn and ignorant condition and gave me sound advice and encouragement.

If the preview was subdued in tone, I had hopes that the sale would be a good deal more lively. But I had much to learn. In the splendid auction rooms the company that gathered round the rostrum was pitifully small considering the size of the catalogue and the importance of the sale. I fear the owner thought so too, as he sat a little to one side and waited for the opening bid, knowing however small the company, there was no drawing back. Again the crimson and gilt-clad lackeys were present to hold the books as they came up for sale. The extremely quiet voice of the auctioneer was hardly audible. I clutched my pencil and strained my none too reliable ears. It was evident that a slight nod of the head, or the flicker of a pencil made the price rise in leaps and bounds and the higher it went, the larger was the ratio of the advance. However, I began to gain confidence as it appeared that Ducharme and I were the chief bidders and as I wanted, for the most part, the books in English and he those in French, we had things pretty much our own way. Then came the Jesuit manuscripts. A small group of priests were present who in a none too lively manner bid against each other for these really valuable records.

I saw by then that the whole sale had been a disaster for Mr. Morin. He told us later that the right people had not been present to bid for the manuscripts. When the sale was over the bulk of the books returned to Canada, divided fairly evenly between Ducharme and myself. But to end this account on a more cheerful note, I must add that Mr. Morin's ardour for collection was not by any means extinguished by this affair. He has lived to issue three excellent catalogues and during the twenty-seven intervening years has added considerably to his vast collection.

That was my sole experience of a New York sale. The depression descended upon the country, and the American Art Galleries, Anderson Galleries disappeared from the scene.

Authors for very good reasons do not as a rule collect books. They either use their imagination or the reference libraries, probably both. I, therefore, did not number many of them among my clients. But it was through one of my Maritime bookbuyers that I came to know Charles G. D. Roberts in the last years of his life.

To be told, in the middle of a business letter, that the writer has three hundred feet of peonies in bloom and he wishes you could share their beauty with him is apt to make you fill his order with unwonted ardour. Just such a letter writer was Mr. William Macdonald of Sydney, Nova Scotia. Moreover, he frequently added some interesting book gossip. For instance, in a letter before me he tells me he has some rare Roberts titles and wonders whether the poet would sign them for him. Then he goes on to say, "In 1920, I was living in Ottawa and one morning on my way to my office I met Mr. Abbott of Thorburn and Abbott book store who told me to come in that afternoon to inspect the library of the late John Reade. I don't think I ever saw a more inviting lot of books. I bought $300 worth. As I had no room for them in my home I had to store them. Unfortunately, most of them were destroyed by fire and ever since the thought of fire terrifies me. There is no worse calamity."

This was prophetic. Many years later Mr. Macdonald

decided to give his large library, while he still lived, to an institution in which he took a great interest, and not long after I was dismayed to read that this place had been completely gutted by fire, including the valuable library.

Mr. Macdonald's letter gave me fresh light on the curious career of John Reade, an early writer of Canadian verse. He is chiefly remembered as the author of *The Prophecy of Merlin and other Poems* (Montreal, 1870) a somewhat rare volume which had come my way from time to time. Reade was an Irishman and on coming to Canada first studied law and then in 1864 was ordained a clergyman in the Church of England. A few years later he left the church to become literary editor of the *Montreal Gazette* and for many years contributed a column under the initials R.V. He became a widely known literary character and was one of the charter members of the Royal Society of Canada. Now we know on good authority that he may be counted among the elect as a discriminating book collector. It was pleasant to be able to send Mr. Macdonald a copy of one of Percy Ghent's all too few contributions to Canadian letters, a small brochure called *John Reade and His Friends,* now, alas, rarely seen.

To follow up Mr. Macdonald's request to get Roberts' signature I set out with a bag full of his books to see if the now aging author would be willing to sign them for my client. Charles G. D., as he always insisted on being called, was then living at the top of an apartment house on Sherbourne Street, with two large mat-like cats. How they managed I do not know for by that time both Roberts and the cats seldom tackled the long flight of stairs. He was charmed to see some of his half-forgotten books and confessed his own collection was far from complete. It was much like watching a father greeting his prodigal sons. I took along one of my own Roberts, given me by an admirer in 1905. (In those Edwardian days gifts from young men were strictly limited to books and flowers.) *The Book of the Rose* was published in June, 1903, by L. C. Page and Co., Boston. On the half title page Roberts wrote:

Dear Mrs. Hood:

I'm glad you have this little book. It is a rare first and only separate edition. I do not possess a copy myself so I envy you.

Charles G. D. Roberts

He signed all of Mr. Macdonald's books readily and later when I came with a much larger collection belonging to Dr. Clarence Webster of Shediac, New Brunswick, I had the pleasure of telling him that the generous doctor was making a library in his honour at Beauséjour. In order to find out how this library was progressing I wrote lately to Mr. H. C. D. Dixon, custodian of the Fort Beauséjour National Historic Park. He told me he had worked with Dr. Webster in the Museum where Sir Charles paid frequent calls. He considers their collection of Roberts' titles is complete, and adds the books are all autographed.

At eighty-three Roberts was busy helping with details of his own biography which Miss Pomeroy had been writing for nine years and planning a volume of his own essays to be published later. This latter volume has not so far appeared.

The early poetry of Roberts, Carman, Sherman and others of that group, when I entered the field in 1928, was considered rare, and commanded higher prices than the works of any other Canadian poets. Even as late as 1936, in my sixteenth catalogue, I listed twelve first editions of Roberts ranging from $20 for *Orion* (Phila.,

1880); *Ave* (Tor., 1892), at $16 and so on. Of Carman's I had even more to offer, eighteen volumes including *Low Tide* (N.Y., 1893), $25; *Poems,* two large volumes, in wrappers, signed by John Murray at $45. Francis Sherman came next with seven volumes, the rarest and most expensive being *Matins,* one of twenty-five copies at $20. It must be remembered that twenty years ago the dollar value was much greater than at any time since. Never again, however, while I was in business, could such prices be asked. I had begun to see the modern trend even at that time. Fortunately, there remained a few faithful followers of these poets and their books filled gaps in many poetic collections.

Some years later I bought a box of books "sight unseen" from a Winnipeg scout. The sender told me he had found it at an auction sale of the contents of a storage company. When I examined the books I had the guilty feeling of an intruder. Here was a collection of the earliest efforts of the little group of poets who called themselves the "Kingscroft Circle." Carman and Hovey, the brothers Charles and Goodridge Roberts and "Nain," their sister, were the moving spirits. These books and pamphlets, signed and given to each other, were the cherished possessions of "Nain." As Mrs. Macdonald she had moved to Winnipeg where ill health and death had early overtaken her. The treasured records of long ago had been put into storage, never to be reclaimed. These relics of the "Music Makers and Dreamers of Dreams" seemed to cry out to be possessed. If there is a happy ending, it is that they fell first into my hands and through me into the possession of those who valued them.

Canadians for well over a hundred years have been persistent and undiscouraged poets and rhymers. An endless flood of small books of verse flowed from the local presses of the country, good, bad, serious and amusing. Most of the libraries and collections I bought seemed to include some of these poetic efforts and gradually the shelves allotted to them became crowded and space had to be found in storage rooms. Only the highlights among them, and there were some real poets, could be listed in my printed catalogues. A sudden inspiring phrase came into my mind, "One Hundred Years of Canadian Poetry." I then and there decided to issue a mimeographed catalogue under that title. It was an immediate success and the demand was so great for copies of it that I only kept one for my own records. While it reduced my supply of poetry to a great extent, the shelves did not long remain empty.

It may have been this catalogue that attracted the attention of the librarian at Brown University in Providence, R.I. to Canadian poetry, for it was about this time that I became their agent to supply them with out of print and current Canadian poetry. A fund has been provided at Brown to build up a complete collection of North American poetry and I was told the Canadian section has been much neglected. There was one stipulation only – I was to keep a record of all the titles I submitted. This was simple and proved an interesting record, though there were times when I had misgivings as to the value of some of the 1,200 books and pamphlets that I poured into the apparently endless shelves of Brown University Library.

I do not pose in any way as a critic of Canadian poetry. I write merely from the bookseller's point of view. There are inspired poets in Canada, but the demand is small for their works. Nevertheless, anthologies have been quite popular, even as long ago as sixty or seventy years.

The poetry collection of Victoria College is probably

the most representative one in Canada. This was built up through the generosity and the good taste of the late C. C. James until his untimely death in 1917.

Among my tools when collating and dating Canadian literature, and especially poetry of the past seventy-five to one hundred years, was the small paper-covered volume issued by the University of New Brunswick in 1935 called *A Catalogue of the Rufus Hathaway Collection of Canadian Literature.* This collection represented the passionate interest of one ardent admirer of Canadian letters and especially of the work of Carman, Roberts, Hovey and their contemporaries, including Lampman and F. G. Scott and Duncan Campbell Scott, to name only a few. Printed works, manuscripts and reviews were hoarded and later, because Hathaway so desired, were presented to the University of New Brunswick. It was a difficult collection to catalogue but in spite of some confusion I always found it useful in determining the chronology of some books of Canadian literature and especially those of Roberts and Carman. Another book which shows the interest in Canadian poetry in the 1920's is a curious one by Edward S. Caswell, *Canadian Singers and their Songs, a Collection of Portraits, Autograph Poems and Brief Biographies* (McClelland & Stewart, 1925). There are one hundred and four poets listed in the index, and each one is represented by a portrait and a poem in the author's handwriting—a really amazing effort and one which the editor himself calls "arduous." The book went into three editions and is, therefore, not difficult to come by. The editor's library, or perhaps only part of it, fell into my hands later on. Most of the much-loved books had been beautifully rebound in morocco, tooled with great taste. This treatment would be scorned by dyed-in-the-wool first edition collectors, but there is something to be said for those who long to see their treasures given bindings fitted to their worth.

Writing of New Brunswick collectors and authors has reminded me of a famous if somewhat erratic customer. At irregular intervals throughout my files appear brief letters ending with an almost illegible signature of one word. This after some guesses we decided was "Beaverbrook." Among other distinctions Lord Beaverbrook remained the only Baron on our mailing list. His letters I am compelled to record were greeted with groans from the members of the staff who had to deal with his multitudinous places of residence. With the first snowflakes and the opening of the Royal Winter Fair Lord Beaverbrook took up his residence at the Royal York Hotel in Toronto. Then began a series of early morning telephone calls and a hurry-up order to send down to the hotel for his inspection a pile of books he had ordered months ago for the library of the University of New Brunswick. Our chief difficulty in our dealings with his Lordship was what might be termed, with no romantic connotations, the eternal triangle. The Book Room and the University of New Brunswick formed the two solid sides, with Lord Beaverbrook the wavering third, as he moved from New York to Nassau, to Jamaica and back to London. Our quotations and bills followed him on these rounds and took months to reach him. Why, we often wondered, should a man of such marked ability for business conduct our small transactions with him in such a casual manner? Once while he was in Toronto, he paid us a call. It was, of course, interesting to meet the dynamic man who among other achievements, when no longer young, had organized the production of air craft necessary for the Royal Air Force at the beginning of the second World War. His first remark on entering the Book Room was, "Are these all the books you have?" I replied with some dignity, I hope, "We go in for quality, not quantity, you will find, I think."

Though his knowledge of Canadian books is limited, he has a strong sense of the value of libraries to the community and besides his interest in the University library at Fredericton he has established smaller libraries in other parts of the province. In spite of his long residence in England it is noticeable that he has never lost his Canadian accent.

My correspondence with Lawrence Burpee extended over many years and was so friendly and congenial one would have thought we knew each other well, while the sad truth is we had never met. His life was dedicated to the advancement of information about Canada. He was steeped in Canadian history and used his facile pen to interest others in it by writing books and contributing articles to historical and geographical publications, many of which he actually founded. But perhaps the subject closest to his heart was the tremendous saga of the search for the Western Sea. These rhythmic words were used for the title of his best known book in 1908. By the time I came on the scene *The Search for the Western Sea* was twenty years old and had attained the distinction of being a collector's item. A little clumsy in appearance for one volume and yet not quite big enough for two, it contained between its covers just what the title suggested in a delightful and orderly manner. This had never been attempted before and it appeared at a time when Canadians were beginning to show a little curiosity about western adventure. The 1,000-copy edition was soon exhausted.

In my fifth catalogue issued in 1931, I listed this book, with a good deal of wordy fanfare, at $45, a really high price at that time for a book only twenty-four years old.

The demand for it must have been insistent for in spite of the depression, Macmillan & Company issued a new and revised edition in two volumes in 1935. This did not kill the value of the first edition since by that time it had entirely disappeared from the market.

When Mr. Burpee's accumulation of books threatened to engulf him, he would send me lists, with a generous note saying, "Send me whatever you consider they are worth to you." In the autumn of 1947 a long list of most desirable books arrived with a cheerful note to say he was about to fly to England to see his daughter, Mrs. Lowe, wife of the Dean of Christ Church, Oxford. I sent the cheque at once wishing to have the transaction concluded before his departure. A week or so later we were shocked to hear of his sudden death a few hours after his arrival in England. I have thought since he might have had a premonition of the end and was anxious to have some of his treasured books go into the hands of those who would value them.

It was a privilege later, as an appreciation of his work, to help Mrs. Burpee in the final disposition of his large library.

There was little monotonous regularity about our business day. The morning post invariably provided some surprises: a letter from someone in Bechuanaland asking for a geological memoir on our Haliburton district; a polite request from a Japanese professor for a list of publications dealing with Arctic ice; an order from an important United States university whose librarian has been asked to build up the Canadian section; a friendly letter from an old customer after a lapse of years giving his new address. Sometimes, of course, there were less pleasant communications, perhaps about a mistake in an order which sent us in a flurry to our files.

Turning over these files, twenty-six years of them carefully wrapped and labelled, I have been reminded of many episodes which made up the varied pattern of our Book Room life.

Romance once invaded the Book Room. A love story of long ago was gradually revealed, a sad tale with no hope of a happy ending, though by chance I was able to bring some consolation to one of the twain. An elderly lady arrived one day and said she had come because she understood I might be able to help her to find some books she particularly wanted. Did I know the books and pamphlets written by a Quebec author called George M. Fairchild, Jr.? I said I knew them well, that he had written six brochures and edited two others. Some of them were fairly easily found, while others were scarce, especially the privately printed and handsomely illustrated one called *The Journal of an American Prisoner at Fort Malden and Quebec in the War of 1812* (Quebec, 1912).

My visitor was intensely interested and asked me to make a search for them as she intended to collect a complete set. She would come back in about a month.

Now George M. Fairchild, Jr., as I knew from my many visits to Quebec, had a strange history. He was born in Quebec in 1854 and finished his education at the University of New York and then went into business there. He must have been an able young man for by the time he was thirty-six he had made enough to retire to Quebec on his means where he married the granddaughter of the Hon. John Neilson, publisher and patriot. Thereafter Fairchild lived the life of a country gentleman collecting a good library of Canadiana, which he later sold, and writing what might be called picturesque local history. For instance, one booklet is called *A Short Account of Ye Quebec Winter Carnival* (Quebec, 1894), and another, *Rod and Run, Rifle and Canoe and Snowshoe in Quebec's*

Adirondacks (Quebec, 1896), and so on. But his income did not keep up with his tastes and gradually diminished until by the time I met him the whole family was living on the memory of past wealth.

He was an extremely handsome man, if somewhat conscious of this, and dressed in a becoming fashion, something between an artist and woodsman. He died under tragic circumstances in 1912.

Gradually I was able to collect the books Mrs. H. wanted and every time she came I had something to show her. As we became friends I revealed my memories of the Fairchild family and she in turn told me something of the romance of her youth in New York in which George Fairchild played the leading role. Although she had never seen him after he left New York, she knew a little about his subsequent history. I asked her one day if she would like to have the address of Mr. Fairchild's one remaining daughter who lived, I knew, a rather solitary life in Quebec. She was delighted and from this sprang a deep friendship and, while they lived, an exchange of visits and an affectionate correspondence.

In her will Mrs. H. left instructions that her now complete collection of Fairchild books should be deposited in the Quebec Archives Building. It fell to our lot to have the brief dedication suitably printed and bound in blue morocco and with this we dispatched the books.

The mysterious forces of coincidence were surely called into play to lead her to my door. No one else could have completely satisfied her desire for the books, and at the same time helped to "knit up the ravelled sleeve" of her romance.

For the most part our customers came in one at a time. This was fortunate because space was limited, partly owing to our inability to keep our floor free from cartons filled with incoming and outgoing books.

Unlike the traditional second-hand bookshop, we harboured no unofficial book club members and perhaps thereby missed some congenial book gossip. But we did sometimes, using a good deal of discretion, put people of similar tastes in touch with each other. On one such occasion a friendship was formed which had far-reaching and significant repercussions.

Professor George H. Needler was one of our welcome visitors from the time of his retirement in 1936 as head of the Department of German at the University of Toronto. Freed from his professional duties he began at once to devote his time to research and authorship. There were numerous subjects in which he was interested and with his background he felt he could add some sidelights of lasting value to our literature. After twenty industrious years he has now, at the end of 1957, produced twelve books of which he is either complete author or editor. Beside all this his contributions to learned periodicals are numerous. The major part of his works has a Canadian atmosphere, but occasionally his knowledge of Scottish and German literature come to the fore.

It was while he was writing his book to be called *Otonabee Pioneers* that my small part in an interesting encounter came to pass. The pioneers in this book were Mrs. Moodie, Mrs. Traill, Mrs. Stewart and others of the environs of Peterborough, Ontario, during the mid-nineteenth century. I was flattered when he asked me to read the *Pioneers* in manuscript and to see if I could locate some descendant of Mrs. Traill who might have a hitherto unpublished portrait of her. It happened that I could.

An occasional and always stimulating visitor to the Book Room was Mr. Eric Duke Scott (he who had so nobly helped us to sort *The Canadian Magazines*). Now I knew that Mr. Scott's wife was a great-granddaughter of

Mrs. Traill, so on his next appearance I told him about Professor Needler's book and his hope of getting an original photograph of Mrs. Traill. Mr. Scott said at once he would get in touch with Professor Needler and there the matter ended as far as my help was concerned. But it was not long before I heard that, despite a difference in their age span, a warm friendship had developed.

The desired portrait of Mrs. Traill was found and appeared in *Otonabee Pioneers* (Toronto, 1953). The book was a great success and was especially welcomed in Peterborough where the Professor was feted and signed many copies. The contact with Mr. and Mrs. Scott sent the author back to his early interest in Sir Walter Scott, and it was not long before he was working industriously at his next book, *Reminiscences of Sir Walter Scott's Residence in Italy in 1832 by Sir William Gell, edited with an Introduction by G. H. Needler with a Portrait by Morani* (Toronto, 1953).

The background of this book needs some brief explanation. I give it with the hope that it may interest others as much as it has me in that a chance encounter of two literary-minded Canadians sent relics of Sir Walter Scott back to a final resting place at Abbotsford.

In the spring of the last year of Scott's life he and his daughter Anne went to Naples. The British Government, in recognition of his greatness, outfitted a frigate and put it at his disposal for the voyage from England. In Italy Scott was much in the congenial company of Dr. Hogg and of the writer and novelist, Sir William Gell, and in spite of his ill-health spent many happy hours examining ancient manuscripts and wandering among the ruins. It was on one of these expeditions that the artist Morani, unknown to Scott, made a sketch of his head and shoulders. Scott returned to England and died in September. Soon after Anne wrote to Sir William Gell, begging him to record his conversation with her father. This Gell did, his manuscript running to about fifty pages. Both Gell and Anne died shortly after and the manuscript and the sketch came into the hands of Dr. Hogg. He in turn left them to his niece who, in the course of time, became the grandmother of Mr. Eric Duke Scott of Toronto. While Mr. Scott was on service during the 1939-1945 War, he visited his grandmother and she, knowing his interest in things literary and historical, gave him the Scott relics.

The portrait in pencil, considered a remarkable likeness, and the Gell manuscript, were examined by Professor Needler on one of his visits to the Scotts and so thrilled him that he asked to be allowed to do extensive research on the circumstances surrounding them. The result was the production of the *Reminiscences* with many more ramifications in the introduction than I can recount here. Lovers of Sir Walter will find this small book interesting for the account of the personalities involved and the description of travel in Italy in 1830, and the reproduction of the portrait.

The final Canadian chapter in the story closed with Mr. Eric Scott's decision to offer the portrait and manuscript to the Scott Memorial Museum at Abbotsford. All the arrangements and correspondence involved in the generous gift were ably undertaken by Professor Needler. So ended a strange course of events set in motion by a few words spoken in the Book Room.

After writing this account I received from Professor Needler his twelfth book fresh off the press in December, 1957, entitled *Louis Riel, the Rebellion of 1885.* This describes his own experiences in the affair, memories of seventy-two years ago. To add to the vividness of the narrative Mr. Scott was able from his collection to contribute an autographed letter of extraordinary interest, written by Riel on May 6, 1885.

It grieves me to think I have told no tales about some of my kindest and most satisfactory customers. For instance, Mr. Ernest C. Oberholzer of Ranier, Minnesota, who was so keen about books on our fur trade and enjoyed, as he called them, my "admirable annotations"; Mr. Oscar Orr of Vancouver, who never failed to order, even during his long and arduous war service; Mr. A. M. Terroux of Montreal, who always seemed to find books he wanted in my catalogues and was responsible for directing many keen collectors to my door; Mr. Arthur Ford of London, Ontario, who has done so much to encourage the study of local history in Western Ontario and whose stories of his trip to Australia in wartime as president of the Canadian Press have long lingered in my memory; Mr. J. B. Bertrand of Fort William, an early client who never deserted me; Mr. Frank Ridley of Toronto, an ardent archaeologist who set himself the task of learning French so that he could read the Jesuit *Relations* in the original; and many, many more.

All I learned from my bibliographical studies and from my years of experience could never compare in scope with the knowledge I gleaned from my customers.

6. Women, Collectors or Writers?

Incredible as it may seem to us now literature was highly respectable in the past and even fashionable.

I expected my customers to be men; and they were, with few exceptions, for women are not collectors. This may seem a severe verdict, but it has been my experience. Women rarely possess that irresistible, consuming passion to possess books that has led men through the ages to build up priceless collections.

Lack of funds they can call their own to use for the purchase of books may have had something to do with the feminine trait, but I think it goes much deeper. When women buy old books, they do so with a purpose, to study a period, to follow a hobby, to trace their ancestors. But looking back over the years I can remember only a few who were informed, fervent and reckless collectors. I hope those who consider themselves collectors will forgive me and will rank themselves with "the few." However, many women love the books they accumulate and read them, and quite unashamed I number myself among these. For instance, in my private library I have gathered (not collected) from time to time a number of delightful "books on books." Among them, of course, are some of Andrew Lang's. Chief of these in my affection is his *Letters to Dead Authors,* now almost in tatters, so often has my copy "heightened joy, cheered my mind in sorrow." But to back up my contention that women are not by nature collectors, I reread his delightful little book called *Books and Bookmen.* Here he gracefully discusses the matter in a chapter called "Lady Book Lovers," and concludes with the remark, "it remains uncertain whether the owners (of these books) as a rule were bibliophiles."

The "book hunger" of one woman has remained vividly in my memory for twenty years. She came from a remote village on the north shore of Lake Superior and asked if she could see my books in the evening as she had to leave for home next day. She had some knowledge of our poets, chiefly Roberts, Carman and Pickthall, and longed to know more. It was flattering to have such a delightful and receptive person eager to absorb anything I had to tell and our talk lasted long into the night. She told me of a difficult day and night journey she had taken once to hear a lecture on Canadian books. At last with a small bundle of books under her arm she reluctantly tore herself away. I hope I was generous for she had little money to spare and I never heard of her again.

We had quite a laugh with one visitor. She came from the prairies where she had been a librarian in a small but active library and was familiar with my catalogues.

"At last!" she sighed as she sank wearily onto one of the hard office chairs. "This is my first trip to the east and the two places I most wanted to see were Niagara Falls and Dora Hood's Book Room."

But if women are frugal and infrequent buyers of books, they are authors of no mean stature and have contributed to Canadian letters elements entirely lacking in the output of their male contemporaries.

I notice in looking through one of my early catalogues I have listed books by three women writers which have become collectors' items. Had it not been for these vivid chroniclers we would have had but a dull and impersonal picture of our past.

As these and other books by women writers passed through my hands, some only once, others many times, I gradually stored up a fund of unusual information on the background of the books and their writers.

I have chosen only a few, perhaps because they appealed to me, though the list could be extended almost indefinitely to the weariness of the reader and the writer.

If we go back to 1769 and the first novel in English with a Canadian background, it is somewhat of a shock to find it a thoroughly frivolous story. The only copy I ever possessed of the first edition of *The History of Emily Montague* was still in wonderfully good preservation. How the four small volumes had remained in close contact all those years is a mystery, one of the many that confront the bookseller. There were two early editions—one in 1769 and another, still in four volumes, in 1777. Then in 1809 came an edition in French, *Voyage dans Canada, ou Histoire de Miss Montaign*—this time four volumes in two. After that there was a long gap of one hundred and twenty-one years before the Graphic Publishers of Ottawa revived the romantic history of Rivers and his divine Emily. The great charm of this revival is the introduction and notes by the late Lawrence Burpee, with an appendix of extracts from the letters and gazettes of the time.

It is well known that the authoress, who did not reveal her identity on the title page, was Frances Brook, wife of the first clergyman of the Church of England in Quebec. Mr. Burpee's account of the young authoress is entertaining. He pictures her as one of a group of writers and actors who counted among their company Richardson, Garrick, Burney and even Goldsmith, and the immortals,

Dr. Johnson and James Boswell. Frances seems to have been an industrious young person ever trying her pen in new ventures. After the departure of her husband to take up his duties in Canada she wrote *The History of Julia Manderville,* and perhaps because in thought she was trying to picture her husband's surroundings she puts into the mouth of one of her characters some wise remarks:

> Canada, considered merely as a possession . . . gives security to our colonies, is of more national importance to us, than all the sugar islands in the globe. But if the present inhabitants are encouraged to stay, by the mildness of our laws and that full liberty of our commerce to which every national creature has a right; if they are taught by every honest means a love for that constitution . . . if they are allured to our religious worship . . . if population is encouraged, the waste land settled and a whale fishery set on foot, we shall find it, considered in every light, an acquisition beyond our most sanguine hopes.

The sentiments are excellent even if the language seems a little pompous, but as Mr. Burpee points out, the whale fishery of today might have disappointed Mrs. Brook, but even she in her wildest flights of imagination could not have foreseen Canada's contribution to the world's wheat supply.

Emily is, of course, fashionably written in the form of letters between all the characters. They shuttle back and forth between Quebec, Silleri, London, Montreal and even Kamaraski, with no noticeable allowance for loss of time on the ocean. Love, returned or unrequited, gossip and intrigue make up the unexciting story. But there are glimpses from time to time of the beauty of the Laurentian scenery, mingled with descriptions of the limited occupations of the English and perhaps French society in the isolated garrison towns.

The writing itself is flowing and even polished in a

way, though lacking in variety. It would be difficult to distinguish which character is writing were it not for the signature at the end of the letters. It is not certain whether she actually wrote *Emily* in Canada, for she seems to have stayed here only about eleven months.

Frances Brook continued to write on her return to England, novels, poetry, plays and even operas, often with disastrous results.

I have taken the liberty of quoting from the Graphic Publishers edition, because it is now long out of print and not easily found. I cannot ask permission to use these extracts, for the publishing house has ceased to exist, as I mentioned elsewhere. It is interesting to find at the end of his introduction that Mr. Burpee acknowledges his indebtedness to another Canadian publication. He says Mr. Charles S. Blue's article in *The Canadian Magazine*, vol. 58, November 21st, helped him greatly in editing the Graphic edition. This is just one more instance of the type of Canadian articles we can find in the files of that old periodical.

It was in 1791 that the energetic and talented wife of the first Lieutenant-Governor of the Province of Upper Canada, Mrs. John Graves Simcoe, reached our shores. Like many another Englishwoman of her time, she sketched as easily as she wrote and never seemed to have been so weary that she could not make entries in her diary or sit down with her pencils and sketch book to record the passing scene, be it the falls of Niagara or some featureless point of pine trees. Fortunately for us she meticulously named and dated every sketch.

Although she was already the mother of six children, two of them companions on her journey, she entered into the winter gaieties of Quebec society with the enjoyment of a young girl. When the time came to begin the long and perilous trip to Upper Canada, she sighed at leaving her newly-made friends and then looked eagerly forward to new adventures. We cannot help but love this courageous woman who writes so uncomplainingly of the discomforts of the long journeys taken in the heat of summer or the bitter cold of winter; who gave dances and dinner parties in tents and sheds, and seemed to enjoy them; and who when the time came to leave Upper Canada forever was able to confide to her diary, "took leave of Mrs. McGill and Miss Crookshank (at York), was so out of spirits that I could not dine with them. I cried all day!" We of this province should be forever grateful to Mr. John Ross Robertson for preserving for us the diary and sketches of Mrs. Simcoe. To list in my catalogue: *The Diary of Mrs. Simcoe, with Notes and Biography by John Ross Robertson, with 237 Illustrations (90 of them by herself), Toronto, 1911*, was to have a shower of eager demands for it. People began to speak of their copies as of prized possessions, along with valued shares and family heirlooms. It had, of course, been long out of print when to the surprise of everyone, a re-issue was announced. This was, except for two slight corrections, the same book, printed from the original plates. No one suspected that they were still in existence. The book had become so rare that even the antiquarian booksellers welcomed the new edition that they could now order at will. This happy situation continued for a few years, then again it was pronounced out of print. The price has naturally mounted, for few owners will part with their copies at any price.

Male diaries we have of this period, but they are dry reading indeed compared to this vivacious woman's.

The city of Toronto is now embarrassed with the possession of a hotel flagrantly misnamed the "Lord Simcoe."

The next outstanding woman writer, in chronological order, was Mrs. Anna Jameson. Perhaps Canadians generally do not realize that Mrs. Jameson was a well-established professional writer long before she published the first edition of *Winter Studies and Summer Rambles,* 3 vols., London, 1838.

This charming edition, on the rare occasions when it does turn up, is sometimes found in the original "brown boards," but more often bound in tooled half calf. The text is a curious mixture. Her frank and unflattering comments on Canadian society as she found it, followed by penetrating accounts of her adventurous journey to the Sault Ste. Marie, is interspersed with her Winter Studies of German literature. Why did she combine two such utterly dissimilar subjects? The answer is in the preface of this edition, perhaps not often read. When she returned to England after two years in Canada she began to prepare the manuscript for publication. At first she considered separating the two subjects, but she says on re-reading her book she decided it would lose some of its character if not issued as originally written. She may have been right from an artistic point of view, but after a hundred and twenty years there are few now who would not skip the *Studies.* The Canadian reader of the original edition, or the later ones which lack the German literature, is grateful that she took such pains to record with accuracy the very things we want to know. In 1852 she brought out another version known as *Rambles among the Red Men.* The intervening years had tamed her pen and she no longer wrote with disparagement of her companions of 1838. It is, however, dull reading when compared with the more spontaneous first edition. There have been a number of modern editions of the Canadian portion of this valuable book, and save the mark! Anna Jameson has now reached television.

Before parting with this author there is one other book of hers I would like to describe. When she was sixty-one she was prevailed upon to bring out a book which she called *A Commonplace Book of Thoughts, Memories and Fancies—Original and Selected.* Part 1, Ethics and Character, Part 2, Literature and Art. With Illustrations and Etchings. London, 1855. All her life she had made a memorandum of thoughts from her own experience, or quotations that appealed to her from the books she had read. These she arranged under headings, separating the passages with delightful designs by her own hand: birds, flowers, angels, dragons. The work grew until it was a formidable volume of 371 pages. I do not know whether the edition was a small one, but I remember only one copy that ever fell into my hands, and it is still there! It is bound in morocco beautifully tooled and most precious in my esteem; it is inscribed on the fly leaf thus: "John Lees Alma from his truly grateful friend Anna Jameson." The Almas of Niagara were the dearest friends Mrs. Jameson possessed in Canada. Thus the volume is a close link with this vivid personality.

Mrs. Moodie's and Mrs. Traill's writings are well known and have been republished many times. There is, however, one book of Mrs. Traill's which can never be reproduced without losing its original loveliness.

Catharine Parr Traill's *Canadian Wild Flowers* will always hold a unique place in Canadian illustrated books. The botanical descriptions were written by Mrs. Traill in her own poetic style with a good measure of Victorian moralizing thrown in which does not detract from the character of the book. The ten exquisite plates were arranged, drawn and lithographed on stone by the clever hand of Mrs. FitzGibbon and finally the whole edition of five hundred copies was hand-coloured by her with great delicacy. In the preface Mrs. Traill adds this interesting note:

> With a patriotic pride in her native land, Mrs. F. was desirous that the book should be entirely of Canadian production, without any foreign aid and thus far her design has been carried out; whether successfully or not remains for the public to decide.

"Mrs. F." was the niece of Mrs. Traill, the daughter of her sister, Mrs. Moodie, and in later editions of *The Wild Flowers,* after her second marriage, her name appears on the title page as Mrs. Chamberlain.

It might be interesting to collectors to know that the first edition was published by Lovell in 1868 and that the gracefully entwined wild flowers on the title page were left uncoloured. In the next edition, 1869, the title page is delicately coloured. It may be imagination only on my part, but I always consider that the plates in the first edition are more beautiful than in any of the later editions. The quality of the paints used may have something to do with this. The book is folio size and most copies are bound in green cloth, though I have seen a few in dark brown.

In the third edition the plates are reversed and in the fourth of 1895 the lithograph lines are much heavier and the colours harsh. Sad to relate the plates are sometimes removed for framing—a desecration to my mind. Picture dealers have told me that there are no finer flower plates than these early efforts of two pioneer Canadian women.

It is probable that newly-arrived English families sent home copies of the *Wild Flowers* to friends in England, and gradually in the course of time they found their way to the secondhand market. This may account for the good fortune I had to get four copies from England, a real find when they were appearing here only at very long intervals.

One of my clients, Dr. Burnette of Ottawa, was an ardent collector of everything pertaining to the Strickland-Moodie-Traill connection and the group of pioneers who settled in and about Lakefield. It was seldom I was able to find the kind of material he wanted. But I learned never to despair and was rewarded by acquiring a long letter written by Mrs. Traill in her extreme old age. One sentence of it I remember ran like this:

"I have outlived all my clever sisters and my brother and am now left with only memories of the past." With the letter came a book of pressed wild flowers made by herself for the pleasure of giving it to some child of her acquaintance. The specimens were faded and brittle and mostly beyond recognition. I wrote to my collector a full description of the book and a few days later found him in the office. He had come to fetch the book. Not for anything, he explained, would he have risked sending it through the mail.

Mrs. Francis Stewart, a contemporary and friend of Mrs. Traill, was a naturalist and a prolific writer of journals and letters. These were cherished by her daughter Eleanor Susannah Dunlop and published in 1889 by the Gazette Publishing Company of Montreal under the appropriate name of *Our Forest Home.* Later, as more records turned up, a second and much enlarged edition was published in 1902. Both were privately printed and intended for the ever-growing family of descendants, but a few copies found their way to the Book Room and were always eagerly snapped up by the collectors. This book probably gives a truer account of the daily struggles with pioneer conditions than we find in the more literary efforts of the Strickland sisters.

There is need now for a new book on the complicated annals of the Canada Company. Much has come to light since the two Miss Lizars, with rare percipience, gathered enough material from letters, diaries and newspapers to fill a plump book they called *In the Days of the Canada Company* (Toronto, 1896).

The Canada Company was founded in 1824 as a colonization scheme and the name is generally linked with the largest settlement known as the Huron Tract, although there were smaller settlements in other parts of Upper Canada.

It was through this Company that John Galt came to Canada as superintendent in 1826. Although he was the chief promoter of the scheme he, unfortunately, fell out with his board of directors and was recalled in 1829. Even in the few years he was here his rugged personality left an indelible mark on the country. Two of his sons later came to Canada and founded the distinguished Canadian family of that name.

As a diverting work of local history, *In the Days of the Canada Company* has held its own for a great many years. The haphazard arrangement of its contents has been criticized but it may have been a difficult task to weld the scraps of local hearsay into a connected story. The joint authors must have considered it a success for the next year they brought out another book called *Humours of '37. Grave, Gay and Grim Rebellion Time in the Canadas* (Toronto. 1897).

There was evidently a well-developed streak of humour in the family, perhaps inherited from their father, David Home Lizars, a judge of the county of Perth and a veteran of '37. When a young man he was a member of Capt. Luard's volunteers of '37-'38 and not being impressed with the record of the company, young Lizars named it the "Bloody Useless."

By the time *The Valley of the Humber* (Toronto, 1913) was written, one of the sisters had married and Miss Katherine alone seems to have been responsible for this delightful book. All these books add much to our storied local history and we cannot help but be grateful that they were written with such a light hand.

I made an excursion one summer to the Huron Tract, determined to find records of early settlers and possibly some original documents issued by the Canada Company itself.

Mr. Gavin Green's shop was my first port of call. It was filled, and the collection of old furniture, stoves, garden, farm and household implements overflowed onto the sidewalk. At the open door, looking absurdly like Abe Lincoln, stood Mr. Green himself. I introduced myself and it was not long before I found that he was even more a bookman than he was a furniture dealer. Out of a drawer he produced a handful of the most perfect copies of the little paper-covered First Reader, Part I, I had ever seen. Not many of them have survived the hard use they were put to by their small owners. These were part of the original stock of some village shop and had never reached the little red schoolhouse.

For years Mr. Green had attended every auction sale in Huron County and had unearthed many interesting treasures in this occupation. He had remarkably good taste and his shop was kept in immaculate condition by his wife. She had very little use for the antique but less for dust and rust and her hours on duty in the shop were occupied applying black lead and beeswax and turpentine. It was natural then that Mr. Green found a collection of books and papers difficult to conform to his wife's idea of a tidy shop, and for domestic peace had removed these wares to the garage attached to his house.

I was invited to lunch with the couple and from there to inspect the books.

The house was an amusing combination of the taste of two very different people. Mrs. Green liked everything new and up-to-date, while he showed me with understandable pride a beautiful example of Baxter's work at its best. His collection of old clocks and early Canadian cabinet-making would have delighted the connoisseur. In 1948, when he was eighty-six, he wrote a book. It was some years after my visit that *The Old Log House and Bygone Days in our Villages* appeared with the imprint, Goderich, Ontario. I know of none better equipped to tell the tale.

I had come prepared for dust and there was plenty of it in the garage, but there was much to make the visit worth while. Canada Company land grants, early township laws, account books of some of the first business operations in the county and maps. The most valuable volumes, of which I now have a record, I listed thus:

Canada Company. Diagrams of the township of Upper Canada, showing lots purchased from H. M. Government by the Canada Company. 2 vols.

Large 4to, full calf. Contains maps: 97 in each volume with crosses showing lots, block and acreage owned by the Company. No date but evidently before 1837, probably 1828.

Fortunately, Mr. Green knew the value of these records rescued by him from oblivion, but he needed the help of someone who could turn them into cash.

I slept well content that night in a vast bedroom in a fine old rambling house not far from the cliffs that overlook Lake Huron. My journey had not been in vain.

In the years that John Galt spent in Canada he

founded three well-chosen centres, Goderich, Guelph and Galt. The story goes that the plans for two of these places became confused and it is evident that the cart-wheel design of Goderich would have been much more suitable for a town in the midst of unlimited land than for one on the very edge of an enormous body of water where the only point some of the streets could lead to was an abrupt escarpment. John Galt built his own house in the townsite of the inland settlement of Guelph, and it was in this place that a book after his own heart was written many years later.

There were two Miss Leslies, of English birth and good education, who in time became the aunts of Col. Baptist Johnston, a well-known figure in Ontario military circles and now Queen's Printer of Ontario. Both these ladies had a taste for writing, confining themselves to the popular mid-Victorian theme of the careers of the kings and queens of England. But, greatly daring, early in the 1870's, Miss Mary Leslie wrote a novel—a murder story. Cleverly, as Jane Austen had done before her, she placed her characters in surroundings she knew well, but with untoward results. She took a male pseudonym and the title read, *The Cromaboo Mail Carrier, by James Thomas Jones, A Canadian Love Story*. Guelph, 1878. Published by J. H. Harding, Guelph, Ontario.

The countryside was minutely described and the characters thinly veiled under false names, but the fat was in the fire when the first sentence declared, "Cromaboo is the most blackguard village in Canada." It was a dramatic start and one cannot help but admire the daring of the young writer. The trouble arose when it became evident as the excellent story unfolded that the place was actually the nearby village of Drumbo.

Alas, poor Miss Mary Leslie! The book, being published locally, at once fell into the hands of her fellow citizens.

An uproar resulted and in distress Miss Mary rushed to the printer and put an end to the distribution of any more copies. Thus only a very few copies have come to light in the past seventy-five years.

Sadly, though perhaps not wisely, she returned to her safer subjects—the lives of the kings and queens.

Indian captivity narratives have always been eagerly collected and read, and they are important since they belong to a definite period in the white man's search for the Western Sea. In the annals of Canada there are only a few written accounts of captivities compared to the number originating south of our borders, where whole catalogues of them sometimes appear.

One of ours is unique on several counts. It is written by two women; it is brief and authentic; it arose out of the North West Rebellion of 1885 and the book bears the rare imprint, Parkdale, Ontario. Moreover, it has an excellent title. It appeared in my fourteenth catalogue and reads thus: *Gowanlock, Theresa and Delaney, Theresa. The Life and Adventures of, or Two Months in the Camp of Big Bear.* Parkdale, 1885, 2 parts in 1 vol., with Drawings. Both women describe the murder of their husbands, before their eyes, at Frog Lake and their painful experiences as captives.

Mrs. Gowanlock was a young bride who arrived at Frog Lake just as the Rebellion broke out. Mrs. Delaney befriended her and together they went through their bitter experience. After the murder of their husbands they owed their lives to the halfbreeds and Wood Cree Indians while they wandered on the prairies until accidently rescued by scouts of the Mounted Police.

I sometimes wondered why the book had been published in Parkdale, at that time a completely separate suburb of Toronto. In looking up the account of the Frog Lake massacre in Dr. C. P. Mulvaney's excellent book on the history of the North West Rebellion (Toronto, 1885), I found that George Gowanlock, one of the murdered men, had two brothers who were the proprietors of the *Parkdale Times*. It was natural then that the little book was eventually put out by this printing press, probably the only book they issued. It would be an interesting exercise in research to look up the file of this newspaper, if one exists, to see what comment appears about the book, or better still, if there is an actual verbatim report by the two women.

Another captivity, though it did not occur in Canada, was responsible for the establishment of a well known family in this country. The diary of the captivity was first published as an appendix in the book by a Canadian woman, known as *Ten Years of Upper Canada in Peace and War 1805-1815* (Toronto, 1895). The author, Matilda Edgar, was the daughter of Thomas Gibbs Ridout, for many years cashier of the Bank of Upper Canada, and granddaughter of the Hon. Thomas Ridout, the subject and narrator of the captivity. Lady Edgar, as she afterwards became when her husband was Speaker of the House of Commons in Ottawa, had a deep interest in the history of her country and a facile pen. Fortunately, the family letters had been preserved and fell into her capable hands. Around them she weaves the story of passing events. "They range," she says in her preface, "over a stirring period and give a faithful picture of an epoch of Canadian history which . . . now has a deeper significance for us Canadians than the contemporary triumphs of Salamanca and Waterloo." The war of 1812 comes vividly to life as we read the letters of the two young Ridouts, one in the army and the other in the navy, addressed to their anxious parents waiting in York. The picture of the times, however, would be incomplete were it not for the accurate and detailed background of the history interwoven by the author.

The captivity takes us further back in history. Briefly, Thomas Ridout had arrived in North America at the close of the Revolutionary War, to be under the guidance of a brother who had settled in colonial Maryland. After a life of extraordinary adventure for some years, he decided to make his way to Kentucky, in company with others, with some thought of settling there. The journey on the Ohio River began as usual in flat boats, the swift current being the only power needed for the voyage. After two days of peaceful travelling, they were suddenly and disastrously attacked by a band of Shawnee Indians and taken prisoners. With the exception of Mr. Ridout, all the travellers were savagely murdered in the days that followed. Unaccountably he was befriended by what he terms a "good" Indian and his squaw. Over and over again when his life was in jeopardy he was protected by these remarkable people. Then began long months of wandering through the wilderness of forest and rivers, stopping at Indian villages and then pressing on he knew not where. At length it became evident that their goal was the British garrison at Detroit under the command of Captain Wiseman of the 53rd Regiment. Here the captive was welcomed and given clothes and money, and as he puts it: "My friends and protectors, the Indians, did not go unrewarded." He travelled with the 53rd to Upper Canada and eventually settled at Newark and York and founded a numerous family. This brief account does not convey the value of the diary, which abounds in vivid pictures of Indian life and customs.

I am tempted here to stray from my original theme of women writers of Canadian books and to recount the discovery of a link with this old diary in a recent book.

In 1947, the Cambridge Press published a small book

called *Journal of Thos. Hughes, for his own Amusement and Designed only for his Perusal by the time he attains the Age of 50 if he lives so long (1778-1789).* I ordered this book, having seen a review which said the author of the journal had been in Canada as an ensign with the 53rd Regiment. I intended only to glance through to get, so to speak, the meat out of it, but soon I found I could not lay it down. The journal is written with frank and boyish charm and tells of his capture by the Americans during the Revolutionary War and his life on parole for four years behind the lines. After the war he rejoined his old regiment in Canada and was stationed at Detroit, and to my astonishment records the arrival at the garrison of "a Mr. Ridout whom the savages had just restored to liberty." He gives an account of the captivity and the kindly welcome of the officers. It is not often that contemporary accounts agree so completely and I naturally turned to a copy of the Ridout diary to see if Ensign Hughes was mentioned there. I was delighted to read Mr. Ridout's remark, "A Mr. Hughes, a lieutenant in the regiment, gave me £10 for my pocket." It was characteristic of Hughes that he made no mention of this kindly act. Sad to relate the young soldier died of consumption at the age of thirty and a hundred and fifty-seven years were to pass before his journal appeared in print.

Lady Edgar, in spite of many duties as mother and hostess, pursued her historical studies throughout her life, and two more books came from her pen. In 1904 she was asked to write the life of General Brock for the *Makers of Canada* series brought out by Morang & Co.; and in 1912 *A Colonial Governor in Maryland* appeared. Two of her children became well known in educational and literary circles: Miss Maud Edgar was the founder of a noted girls' school in Montreal. Dr. Pelham Edgar was for forty years a professor of English literature at Victoria College and the friend and patron of many young and struggling authors; had it not been for his encouragement two young women, Marjorie Pickthall and Audrey Alexandra Brown, might never have enriched our literature with their poetry. He was also responsible for the appointment of E. J. Pratt and, much later, Northrop Frye, to his staff. All three became Fellows of the Royal Society of Canada, and were subsequently awarded the Gold Medal of the Royal Society of Canada, each being successively Head of the English Department at Victoria.

The women writers I have mentioned, nearly all drew from their own experience of life in a new country, and we would be the poorer had they not been inspired to record it for us. There are gaps, however, to be regretted. I know of no outstanding book by a woman of life on the prairies of an early date—let us say, before the advent of the railways.

Two recent books of the early west were written in old age, and, delightful as they are, they can only qualify as reminiscences. Mrs. J. B. Tyrrell's *I Was There* (The Ryerson Press, 1938) is a touching account of the courageous life she lived in the early days of the Yukon with her noted husband, and *For my Children's Children* (Montreal, 1937) by a daughter of Alexander Tilloch Galt, Mrs. Springett, describes her life as a bride of a remittance man rancher on the prairies in the 1890's.

I have before me a copy of a small paper-bound book, now so frail that it has to be tied with string to keep it together, called *From Ontario to the Pacific by the C.P.R.* (Toronto, 1887) by Mrs. Arthur Spragge. The preface explains that the substance of the book came out in the Toronto *Week* during the progress of the journey she relates, and that it supplies an existing deficiency of information about a most interesting part of the country, especially the district of Kootenay, and the mining interests of British Columbia, of which no later account is extant than Mr. Sandford Fleming's *Old and New Westminster.* This is exactly what the collector looks for in local history and so seldom finds. Mrs. Spragge, as the young wife of an engineer working in the mountains, set out in June, 1886, from Toronto to join at Winnipeg the first through train to the Pacific, from Montreal. She describes the rail and boat and again rail journey to Winnipeg a few days before Dominion Day, which had been auspiciously chosen as the day of the arrival of the first transcontinental train. There was a salute by the Winnipeg Field Battery and two military bands and the inevitable crowds. By mistake she was shown into the directors' private pullman and before being removed to more humble regions had a chance to examine the "Honolulu" and to discover that it boasted a three-foot-six bath, a luxury not to be found seventy years later on the much publicized "Canadian." The train journey was the least exciting part of her travelling, most of which was in the saddle along mountain trails. It is a splendid factual little book with a nice balance of description and anecdote to carry the reader along. She uses the names of her companions freely, a relief from the Victorian tendency to hide identity behind initials and dashes. Altogether it was a stirring year to spend in the mountains, but it was not by any means her last. I remember seeing each summer for many years well into the twentieth century a small notice appear in the social column of Toronto newspapers, "Mrs. Arthur Spragge and Miss Spragge have left for their summer cottage at Golden, B.C." Unfortunately, no more books came from her pen.

In all my years as a bookseller, I remember only one woman who collected books by women. And yet this might be quite an absorbing pastime for I can think of many well worth possessing besides the ones I have described.

I have proved, I hope, that while women are not by nature collectors, they have it in them to be something greater, the writers of "collector's items."

7. Talking Shop

The test of a vocation is the love of the drudgery it involves.
—Logan Pearsall Smith

The secondhand book business has a very long history and has had some adherents who have become famous in other ways. It is recorded that Alexander Cruden "maintained himself by keeping a secondhand bookshop" while he compiled his monumental work, the famous *Concordance of the Old and New Testaments.* At times he had periods of lunacy, though whether this was the result of his studies or from worry over the condition of his bookshop, history does not relate He died in 1770 and ever since his name has been a household word, an achievement the rest of us have never attained.

There have been many charming essays and books written about bookshops, real and fictional, but they come for the most part from the able pens of literary book buyers and not from the ever grubby and hard-working hands of the proprietors.

"Handbooks" there are without number on how to conduct most business ventures, but I have never heard of one on how to run a secondhand bookshop. We who drift into the trade develop our own haphazard ways and would, I think, find it difficult to follow rules we had not devised ourselves. What follows, therefore, may not apply to other bookshops but it is the inside story of how we worked.

It took me years to work out a system in the management of routine office work, while ways of buying and selling and writing catalogues came almost by instinct. We had our days of joys and sorrows, of triumphs and humiliations, of ease and drudgery and though the net result in dollars and cents was modest, the life was such a satisfying one that I never dreamed of giving it up. Augustine Birrell in his pithy way wrote, "Never convert a taste into a trade," but I think he was wrong. I would say you must have a taste for books, or you would loathe the trade.

Contrary to the general belief, we are a fairly honest lot. For instance, as we become more expert in our business we actually pay more for the books we buy than we did as novices. Luck it seems is often with the beginner for when I was timid about every outlay I made on books, some wonderful bargains came my way. I have no qualms of conscience on this account, however, for had there been any rival buyer in the field the books would not have become mine. As time went on I gradually built up a firsthand knowledge of the value of a great number of books, both rare and commonplace; I could not in all honesty offer less than I knew they were worth to me. Most of us buy more books than we can handle, and lay out more capital than we should. None of us grows rich!

There is a vast difference between buying a few volumes and estimating the value of a large library. I grew to enjoy the latter, for it required skill and experience with the added possibility of something unusual turning up.

As time went on, and especially after the 1939-1945

War, I did not have so many unorganized collections offered me, such as the Jones and Heyden libraries, for by that time most of the loose collections of papers had been tidied up and unfortunately consigned to the paper drives. The only one of this kind that remained was the Coyne collection and that took me years to acquire although I had known of its existence for some time. The story of it will be told later.

More and more frequently I was called on to price and buy well selected libraries belonging to university professors, civil servants or wealthy businessmen. These books were usually arranged neatly on shelves in attractive libraries or in rather chilly basement playrooms, and the task was much simpler though not as exciting as ploughing through piles of miscellaneous books and papers.

Gradually I devised a method of arriving at a price which developed into playing a little game with myself. I had in time become so familiar with the appearance of a vast number of Canadian books that without even reading their titles I recognized them by the size, the colour of their bindings and other features, very much as we know the appearance of our friends without ticking off each feature. Therefore, when I came into a room full of books I could take a general look at the collection and size up the trend or character of the library. After a few minutes' thought I would jot down on a piece of paper what I thought I should pay for it and put this away in my brief case. Then I would go carefully over the whole collection, putting down in one column on my pad the value of the highlights or really good books on each shelf and in another column a covering price on what I called "run of the mill" books. These included those that turn up frequently and of which I had a good supply and the practically unsaleable others. Often this proved a thoroughly interesting occupation, for when unfamiliar titles turned up I had to spend some time going through them to decide on their value. Then came the final reckoning. The two columns would be added up, the good and the not so good, and putting them together I would arrive at the final price; and here is where the game came in. The original guess would be produced and the two prices compared. In nine cases out of ten they would be within ten dollars of each other! I do not know how I did this and it amused and astonished me over and over again. Though the carefully detailed estimate was probably nearer the real value, I usually gave the seller whichever was higher.

There is one difficult problem which every book dealer has to face. The owners of libraries, almost invariably, will not put a price on their books. Most of them want the dealer to do this and, having got his expert advice, proceed with this as a basis for further bargaining with others. I do not think it occurs to them that this is somewhat unethical. The only method we can employ to offset this is tactfully to explain that the offer must be accepted or rejected at the time it is made and will not be renewed. Sometimes it is very difficult to be so dogmatic. Most bookish people are disarmingly nice and it is distressing to disrupt the friendly atmosphere. The best way is to take the seller into your confidence by explaining that you have many offers of books and must have an answer there and then lest you have too many unsettled offers. Fortunately, I was able gradually to build up a certain confidence in my business ways and my estimates were accepted among those who knew me.

My advice to those who have libraries to sell is to try one of the three following ways of going about it:

1. Try to arrive at a price before you offer your books, keeping in mind that the dealer must make a profit and

that he will have to dispose of the books one by one, while you are to get cash for all without further effort on your part.

2. Make a careful list of your books giving author, title, date and place of publication and exact condition, being sure to find out if all plates and maps are present. Have several copies made and send them simultaneously to the dealers in the community, asking them to quote a price on the lot. Then accept the best. It is not playing the game to withdraw books from the list after sending it out.

3. Go to a dealer you know and trust him if he offers to buy the entire library. This is much less trouble and will probably give you the best return.

I have very happy recollections of buying books from one of my clients of long standing, using quite another method, but I doubt whether it would have worked with anyone else. I had known Mr. W. T. Hunt for years through his pleasant letters and regular orders which came as he moved east from Calgary, Regina, Winnipeg and finally from Niagara-on-the-Lake where he thought he might like to live in his retirement. But the bookshops, libraries and museums drew him like a magnet into the heart of this teeming city. We in the Book Room looked forward to his visits more for the good companion that he was than for his purchases.

I remember vividly one story he told us of his youth in our prairie west. It illustrated the conditions there fifty years ago and brought out the debonnaire ways of the teller. He was in his early twenties when he arrived in Calgary from England with a small amount of capital to invest in the new country. The first step he took was to buy a small property and some cattle and to marry the daughter of a local well-to-do rancher. The young couple were good riders and loved the outdoor life and all went merrily for nearly a year. Then rather suddenly the bottom fell out of the price of cattle and they had to sell and as the land was useless without the stock, they sold that too. When all their debts were paid and he had bought a railway ticket to take his wife back to her father, he had just fifteen dollars left in his pocket. But before putting her on the train he decided to buy her a watch with her name engraved on it. That cost thirteen dollars and fifty cents. Alone now with a dollar fifty in his pocket he walked down the main street of Calgary, and soon met a man he knew slightly.

"What are you doing here, Hunt?" asked his friend.

"Well, I'm broke, sir, and I'm just looking for someone to give me lunch and then I'll try to find a job," replied our friend.

"You don't need to go any further. I'll give you lunch and hire you."

"And that," Mr. Hunt told us with a laugh, "was the last time in my life I ever had to look for work. I stayed with the Northern Electric for the rest of my working days. And my wife still has that watch!"

It is said of Milton that he disposed of his books in his lifetime because he felt he could do so to greater advantage than his widow. This may have been the motive of Mr. Hunt in deciding to part with his collection, but I like to think he knew in selling his books to me they would go to other book lovers. They were all books on the prairie west, well selected, though not excessively rare; for instance there was no copy of *The Red River Settlement by Alexander Ross* (London, 1856) among them. This is the way we went about our transaction. We sat down at the office table, each with a list of the books and decided the price then and there on the merits of each book. It was not a question of me beating down the price or of him trying to get more. He would declare I was offering too much and would never make any money at that rate, while I would reply that the price he had put on them was absurdly low; and the strange part of it was we were both perfectly satisfied with the results. It was a sad day in the office when we read of his death while on a trip to the south.

"He heapeth up riches and knoweth not who shall gather them," as the Psalmist says. The truth of this statement, expressed with such perfection, has often been borne in upon me. It is a peculiar failing of collectors in general not to make some adequate provision for the ultimate disposal of their books. Not that they do not think about them. Many of them have discussed the question with me. Would it be best to leave their books to some institution and thereby assure that they will remain in safe keeping, though perhaps little used or appreciated? Or should instruction be left that they be sold and thus the chance given to other collectors to have the pleasure of possessing them? I know of only a few who have arrived at a definite answer when the "bell tolled".

It has been my somewhat lugubrious duty many times to be called in by widows and asked to value their husbands' books since they knew nothing about them. Some women had exaggerated ideas of the value, while others were willing almost to give them away in order to get rid of such dust-collecting objects.

It is natural and I think wise for a man to enjoy his books to the end of his life, but some moderate idea of their value should be left with sugggestions of how to go about disposing of them. The collector should remember that he will not be present and that the time and the place may greatly alter the possibilities of advantageous sale.

On the whole, widows are generously treated by reputable book dealers.

I have known a few collectors who, like Mr. Hunt, think it wise to sell while they still remain in this fascinating world of books. But here again the exception defies the rule. One of my keenest Arctic collectors decided his end was near and that for the sake of his wife he must dispose of his excellent collection. He issued a lengthy and most desirable list and sent it to three or four of the dealers from whom he had been in the habit of buying. I was the highest bidder and the books arrived beautifully packed to enrich my shelves. Two years later I had a note from the owner asking me to list any of his books I still possessed since he now bitterly regretted having parted with them. I was desolate at the thought of his yearning for his books, but alas, few remained and none of those he wanted.

One young man in his early twenties had, however, solved the problem successfully. He told me, since his parents were quite uninterested in his books and therefore unworthy of them, he had made provision in his will that *I* was to have them, I think gratis!

I cannot hope that I have thrown any light on this vexed question, and since collecting is a habit "half as old as time," it seems possible that men will continue to act in much the same way, regardless of advice.

Booksellers are continually plagued by being asked to quote prices over the telephone. Often it is merely idle curiosity that prompts these calls and most bookmen refuse to give this information. Telephones, as we all know to our regret, are tremendous temptations to some people. I was frequently rung up after business hours by people who were comfortably at home and whose own offices were dark and silent. I remember once answering the telephone late at night to hear a cheery voice saying,

"We have just been having an argument about the value of the first edition of X. . . and someone said Dora Hood was sure to know, so we thought we would ring you up to see who was right." My answer to this was, "That's very flattering, but what time is it at your house?"

On several occasions I was asked to price books for probate, but did not particularly care for this work as the collections often contained quantities of miscellaneous books about which I could only guess. But once I was asked by the librarian of an important university as a business proposition to put a price on a valuable collection of Canadiana. I was not told who had owned the books nor why a price was wanted. It was an interesting piece of work and required a good deal of research as many of the books were extremely rare. Again I applied my own technique of looking over the long list in a casual manner and jotting down an estimate. Then I went seriously to work on it, and as I did not know whether the books were to be sold or donated, I had to use my own judgment and decided to put on them the approximate current price. It took me several weeks to do the work in my spare time. Once again my estimated price and the final detailed amount were within hailing distance of each other, though a good many thousand dollars were involved. I learned later that the books had been left jointly to two heirs. The share of one was given as a gift to the library while the other heir demanded cash. What the final arrangement was I did not hear although I received a letter of deep appreciation from the librarian.

There are so many pleasant aspects of the book trade that it is with reluctance that I write about one sinister side of it. Always present in the mind of the dealer is the possibility of inadvertently buying stolen goods. Perhaps the greatest safeguard against such a catastrophe is to maintain a reputation for fair dealing oneself, so that the disposer of stolen books will hesitate to offer them to you. In older countries, and I reluctantly add, more cultivated ones than ours, there is a larger traffic in stolen books. It is impossible to guard all the valuable books in our libraries and the determined thief will find a way. But the possibility of disposing of them without detection is a problem which may deter the knowledgeable thief. Our Royal Canadian Mounted Police is an astute body and the value of their presence is not fully appreciated. Several times they have called on me when they were tracking down some troublemaker. Unfortunately, one's curiosity is never satisfied, for profound silence is preserved after the interview.

If there ever was any doubt in my mind about the source of the books I was offered, I took the time to have a chat with the vendor, and unless he, or she, was skilled at the art of covering up tracks it was generally an easy matter to get at the truth. Only once did I buy a quantity of books which I discovered afterwards to have been stolen. Nothing could have appeared more innocent than the seller and his surroundings. He was a most presentable young man, neatly dressed and intelligent, who asked me to come to his house and look over the collection he wanted to sell. I went, and found a well-kept and attractive small house in a good, though not a fashionable neighbourhood. There he introduced me to his white-haired, charming, and I believe, quite honest mother. The books were nice, and the owner seemed to know them and their value and was willing to part with them at a reasonable price. The deal went through with friendly gestures on both sides. Six months later I learned to my embarrassment that the books were stolen from a place where the young man was employed in a position of trust.

On the whole second-hand bookmen must have a good reputation for their activities have not been restricted by any uncomfortable bylaws. Once only, for a short period, did we, the dealers, hastily form ourselves into an Antiquarian Book Sellers Association to protect our trade. This was no spontaneous affection for each other, and was out of keeping with our tendency to be "cats that walked by ourselves." Occasionally partnerships have been formed among us, but from my observation they never worked and soon broke up with recriminations on both sides.

On this occasion, however, we were startled into action by a threat from the City Hall that we were to be classed with junk dealers and would be required daily to report all our purchases. We were indignant, and appalled at the prospect of having to list possibly hundreds of books each week.

Our first act was to ask Mr. A. H. O'Brien to be our lawyer and to present our case when it was called. Now Mr. O'Brien was what might be called a "borderline" book seller. During the First War when on leave in London he wisely devoted his time to searching the many bookshops for Canadiana and by 1918 had rather more packing boxes than he had reckoned on. One of his special interests was books by Thomas Chandler Haliburton, judge, author of historical books but more famous as the inventor of the fictional character "Sam Slick." Haliburton's books were great favourites in England and were published there with the exception of four which were first issued in Halifax. So many editions of each were discovered, with the exception of *The Historical and Statistical Account of Nova Scotia* (Halifax, 1829) that Mr. O'Brien later undertook the exacting labour of compiling a bibliography of Haliburton's works. This was published by the Royal Society of Canada in 1919, under the title *Haliburton, a Sketch and Bibliography.* I knew well at one time the ramifications of this bibliography when I laboured to list under their various editions a very large collection of Haliburton's work I had acquired. The demand for these books, especially the Sam Slick series, was somewhat fluctuating and the supply lasted me quite a long time. The other author who especially attracted Mr. O'Brien's attention was George Heriot, whose beautifully illustrated book *Travels in the Canadas,* (London, 1807) has always been a *pièce de résistance* to collectors. When we dealers were in great need of these and other books, Mr. O'Brien could be persuaded to sell them to us "at a price."

Happily, then, we were able to enlist Mr. O'Brien as our champion before the city fathers. We knew that they would not have a chance if they once allowed our fluent lawyer to have his say, for all of us at one time or another had suffered under the onslaught of his torrent of words; and we were right. Our case was so convincingly handled that we were quickly declared free from the crippling bylaw. As we emerged on the City Hall steps our membership in the Toronto Antiquarian Book Sellers Association fell like a discarded mantle from our shoulders and we once more took up our individual cat-like roles. It must be recorded, however, that we collected a modest honorarium for our stalwart beetle-browed attorney.

It was not until 1951 that I had the honour to become a charter member of the Canadian Retail Bookseller's Association. It is a pleasure to record that had it not been for the years of almost unaided work Mr. Roy Britnell had spent on our behalf the Association would never have come into being.

It is said that Gladstone in writing to Bernard Quaritch made this curious observation: "Book collecting may have its quirks and eccentricities, but on the whole it is a vitalizing element in a society honeycombed by several sources of corruption." Quaritch was one of the most successful members of our trade and probably agreed with his correspondent through his long and intimate contacts with book collectors throughout the world. It is, however, axiomatic that the books and the collector must be brought together, and what follows is my experience in that exciting and difficult adventure.

Next to the stock of books on my shelves I considered my mailing list to be the most valuable asset I possessed. It took years to build it up and it never remained static.

It is simple enough to card index all the universities in Canada and to add to these the institutions of learned societies, the Legislative, Public and Special Libraries, and so on. Not all of these, by any means, will read your catalogues and fewer still will buy, but most of them will file them carefully away for reference. Though it took a great deal of resolution, I found it wise to continue to send my catalogues to those librarians who did not order. Eventually, I argued, they would be asked for some out-of-print Canadian book and my name would be familiar to them. But before this happened I found collectors were coming to me through the kind offices of these very librarians. If I failed to show sufficient gratitude at the time I hope this acknowledgment will reach them. In smaller communities librarians are called upon to supply information on a wide variety of subjects. Frequently it seemed people with books to sell were also given my address and I cannot blame the librarians if practically every British newcomer to Canada arrived with a very old (1850!) family Bible and a volume of Robert Burns' poetical works in his trunk. After a generation in this country they were willing to part with them for Canadian dollars. We even contemplated having a post card printed: "We regret to say we do not buy old Bibles or Burns' poems."

The United States libraries, however, presented a problem through sheer vastness of numbers. The educational institutions possessing large libraries make the task of selection a very difficult one but I gradually built up my list from the outstanding names of which I had some knowledge and added others as requests came in for books from Canadian professors and students teaching or taking post graduate work in American colleges. Apart from these institutions I built up a valuable list of private collectors in the United States. Many of these came to me as mysteriously as did manna of old.

Among the tools any book dealer will find useful, at least in the early period of his career, are the book trade papers such as *The Publishers' Weekly.* There are a number of them in the United States and England to choose from. These papers are for the most part published weekly and contain many pages of advertisements for "Books Wanted" and a few for "Books for Sale." Librarians and collectors as well as book dealers use these pages and while not much Canadiana is asked for or offered, I found them useful in building up my mailing cards. *The Publishers' Weekly* ran a column in which new catalogues of rare and out of print books were listed. This I found an excellent source of new customers when my catalogues appeared there, even if some of those who wrote for them were merely curious to see what kind of a catalogue a woman would produce. Through this periodical I actually won a prize for one of my catalogues. Another feature of this periodical was the monthly article on "Rare Books," usually written with a great deal of charm and knowledge. I thoroughly enjoyed reading this and know that in my first few years it gave me an insight into the labyrinthine ways of book collectors. The "Books Wanted" are always numerous and show the penchant of the American public to acquire a wide range of books. Occasionally I advertised in these papers for books I needed but the time and trouble expended in getting books through the customs proved to be unprofitable. As time went on I found my hours too precious to be spent pouring over these lengthy columns and finally I gave up subscribing to this type of periodical.

Since 1950 there has been a courageous attempt to carry on a book search periodical in Canada but it is still in its infancy.

For a good many years my largest orders came from the United States. Librarians and collectors showed their interest in my catalogues by ordering from them regularly. While it distressed me to see so much of my valuable Canadian stock going out of this country year by year, I had no choice in the matter for, except for a few Canadian librarians who never failed to order, such as the University of Toronto librarian, and those of Queen's and McGill Universities, I might not have continued to exist. It never occurred to me to go, for instance, to Dr. Locke, Chief Librarian of the Toronto Public Library, and to say, "Do you not want some of the rare Canadiana I have to offer? Why do you not check my catalogues as assiduously as you check those from England and the United States?" It was not until Miss Marie Tremaine became head of the Reference Library that I received any orders from that source. From then on until I retired a steady stream of orders and requests came in.

Gradually the tide began to turn and not only did Canadian librarians order regularly, though frugally as befitted their budgets, but collectors throughout Canada increased in number and demands for my catalogues were widespread.

It is one of the unsolved mysteries of bookselling, from the Canadian point of view, why the British universities and learned institutions take so little interest in Canadian books. Year after year I dispatched my catalogues to the leading universities in the British Isles with no results.

Apart from Rhodes House in Oxford, the Royal Empire Society, and the University of London, a general silence prevailed. Our history, our economics, our literature, our aborigines, our explorations interested neither librarians nor collectors. I do not think this lack of interest could be attributed to the depression or the war. It never had existed, and this is strange for the British are without doubt the greatest readers in the world. On the other hand, many of the basic early books on what is now Canadian territory were published in England and France and command high prices when they come up for auction in London. It is significant, however, that some of the important British antiquarian dealers maintain offices in New York and price their catalogues in dollars and cents.

Perhaps I have stressed too much the reluctance of some of the public to appreciate the rich fare of Canadiana I laid before them. This is in contrast to the eagerness of those others who made my life as a bookseller so interesting and fruitful. I owe it to these numerous and ardent buyers that not once did I consider a catalogue to have failed. No matter what catastrophe the world in general was enduring at the moment (and, looking back, there seems to have been a long succession of upheavals), a steady stream of orders came by letter and telegram, and best of all by personal calls.

I decided, at one stage, to explore the vast field of advertising. The daily papers I soon found were useless for my purpose. A small notice announcing a new catalogue in a weekly paper, such as *Saturday Night* in its palmy days, could always be counted on to produce clients with comfortable bank accounts, who had come to that period in their lives when they could indulge themselves in a long suppressed desire to buy books. For a number of years my advertisement appeared in the *Canadian Historical Review* where it must have become familiar to librarians and professors, though few mentioned it when asking to be put on my mailing list.

While I was still an amateur at the game I was invited by the librarian of Queen's University to share, with Georges Ducharme of Montreal, the advertising space on the back cover of the catalogue of the Douglas Library being prepared in 1932. This was an honour and fitted in well with the work Ducharme and I did, and I was proud to see the announcement of my business occupying half a page of a booklet that would have a wide circulation. The catalogue is still available (in 1957) and the title reads thus: "Canadiana 1698-1900 in the possession of the Douglas Library, Queen's University, Kingston, Ontario" (86 p.). It is an interesting addition to the bibliophiles of Canadian pamphlets, books, and manuscripts. There is a preface by Dr. Lorne Pierce well worth reading for the light it throws on some peculiarities of the Canadian book situation. For instance, Dr. Pierce says, "It is eminently fitting that the first University in Canada (Queen's) to publish such a bibliography should be the one which established the first chair in Canadian history." He goes on to praise the foresight of Dr. Adam Shortt who realizes the importance of a collection of Canadiana at Queen's in the early nineties. Many years later it was my privilege to journey to Ottawa especially to inspect and finally purchase a quantity of fine pamphlets and periodicals belonging to Adam Shortt. It is well known now that Dr. Pierce added greatly to the Queen's University collection, but the story of this belongs elsewhere in this narrative.

I had, of course, chosen a highly-specialized field in the general business of selling out-of-print books. In time I learned that while book collecting is indigenous in most countries, a taste for Canadiana is sporadic in Canada as elsewhere. When I accepted this fact it was evident that my own catalogues were the best form of advertisement.

Books and a mailing list were important but the very life blood of the business was the catalogue. No one who has not compiled a catalogue can have any idea what a time-consuming task it is. Many of the famous dealers in old books do not write their own catalogues but hand this most delightful work to some trusted employee with a knowledge of the background of books. Bernard Quaritch who had in his fifty years of bookselling (1856-1899) the most extensive trade in the world, did not write his own famous catalogues. He employed Michael Kerney to do this and always gave him due credit for his labours.

It did not take me long to establish certain important principles in compiling a catalogue, the first one being that it is unprofitable to have fewer than 500 titles in a printed list. Mine ranged from this number to 1,200. Another fundamental that I tried to adhere to was that each catalogue should have a fresh appeal and books, no matter how good, should not appear with monotonous regularity. Of course, some books had to be repeated at intervals, not just because they were handy or numerous but because they were wanted and found ready buyers. With these and other ideas in view I always began to build up each catalogue from material I had acquired since the last was issued, perhaps stressing one particular subject if I had been lucky enough to come across a distinctive collection. This was fairly simple since I never put new stock on my shelves before I had card indexed and priced it. This little habit did not make for scrupulous tidiness and will explain to anyone who remembers the Book Room the piles of books whose permanent home seemed to be on the floor. But when they did reach the shelves I knew they were properly priced, a most important rule in any bookshop.

After new material had been exhausted, the list was

filled in with books that had not appeared in at least three previous catalogues. They, too, of course, had to fit into the general character I had decided upon. Title, date and place of publication had to be stated correctly, and if the condition was other than "good secondhand," it must be accurately described. I confess I was apt to describe more fully the contents of books than is often done, but I still think this made my catalogues more useful to the newer collectors than other lists I have known. At first I listed books alphabetically so that it was necessary to read through the whole of it for fear of missing something. Later on I classified the books under appropriate subject headings such as Arctic, Travel, Biography and so on and for this was congratulated by an observant librarian. But from my own experience I do not think it made any difference in the number of books sold, and am convinced my clients read the catalogue straight through from cover to cover.

There is still another feature of compiling a catalogue which must be mastered.

Book buyers who live far from big centres of population must perforce buy from catalogues. Fortunately for booksellers, plenty of people thoroughly enjoy selecting their books this way. There is in it the same element of good or bad luck as there is in the sport of fishing. To encourage these valuable buyers a cataloguer should give an accurate description of each book and from this habit has arisen some inescapable jargon. This must be written into every catalogue, so that it is important for buyers to know the meaning of a few of these obscure terms.

Sir Arthur Quiller-Couch devotes a chapter to the word "jargon" in his delightful book, *The Art of Writing.* In this he deplores the clichés, conventional stereotyped phrases, found in the pages of official and journalists' reports and exhorts his readers to avoid them at all cost. I agree with him heartily, although often guilty of the crime. But the dictionary describes "jargon" as "the peculiar phraseology of a party or sect," and that definition is adopted by us the cataloguers. We are at least brief and when the reader knows the meaning of each word a great deal of expensive verbosity is spared us. The terms are sometimes abbreviated.

In the following list, the only two I thoroughly dislike are "item" and "mint." They are, nevertheless, generally accepted.

Item—a separate article, book, etc.

Mint—perfect as if freshly arrived from the press. (From *Moneta,* a surname for Juno at whose temple in Rome money was coined—hence mint).

Uncut—the leaves are untrimmed—not sheered off by binder's knife.

Unopened—the leaves have not been separated by a paper knife, indicating the book has not been read.

Boards—cardboard covers. In many cases this is the original binding and some collectors prefer this to handsome bindings done later.

Half morocco—the back is bound in leather with cloth or marbled board sides.

Unbound—the book is sewn, with or without plain paper covers.

Wrappers—printed paper covers. These are sometimes "bound in" when a cloth or leather binding is added.

Half title—on a separate page, before the title page, the name of the book appears without any other information. Important in rare books and sometimes removed because it had the former owner's name on it.

Tipped in—instead of maps and illustrations being bound in they are sometimes glued in by the tip or edge of paper.

Shaken—I used this word for a book that was loose in its covers or where the sewing had become loose, but if the sewing is broken this should be noted.

A.L.S.—autograph letter signed.

Foxed—this is a fungus growth in the paper of mysterious origin. It usually appears on pictures but sometimes also on the text. Where there is much foxing it should be noted.

There are numerous others, but these are the ones most used in describing books. All my catalogues bore a brief notice: "All books 8vo (octavo) and in good secondhand condition except where noted."

When I had divided a large catalogue into a number of headings I gave an alphabetical list of these on the inside of the front cover.

After several weeks of concentrated work on the catalogue the cards were ready for the final checking. Then came the last curiously difficult job of correctly numbering each item. Any slip in the task would lead to confusion when the orders began to come in.

Invariably I felt limp at this final stage but a walk to the printers in the fresh air with my manuscript in my brief case usually completely restored me.

For the first ten years the printing was done by the University of Toronto Press. Monotype was used as this made corrections simpler. I always thought the catalogue looked nice, though some of my colleagues said I was too conservative in my choice of covers. Year after year these were the same except for the colour, but I think my customers grew familiar with the make-up and format and welcomed them like old friends. The authorities at the Press allowed me to go behind the scenes and I learned much about the various processes. I enjoyed watching the skilled men at their work and acquired a taste for the smell of printer's ink.

Instead of being elated as I should have been once the effort of writing the catalogue was over, I went through a miserably depressed period. I was convinced that this one was no good, dull, lacked sufficient highlights and so on. Fortunately, this state lasted only a few days and by the time the galley proof arrived I was able to face the future with my usual optimism.

Sometimes there was a long wait before the press returned the finished product. But there was plenty of work for the office staff. Fifteen hundred to two thousand newspaper wrappers had to be accurately addressed, part of them typed and the more permanent list put through the old addressograph which I bought secondhand at a low price; it is still in use after twenty years and is now quite a curiosity.

After the final effort of rolling up and despatching the catalogues we relaxed and awaited with eagerness the arrival of the orders. For many years among the first we received would be a post card signed "Louis Blake Duff." With unfailing good taste he would single out the titbit in the Ontario local history section.

This was now our harvest-time. It was fun to see our postman enter into the game as he counted out the pile of letters in each mail. Telegrams and long distance telephone calls added to the excitement. At first local customers were slow to call and were inclined to be annoyed when they found the books they wanted had been sold. I could only tell them tactfully that the books had been on the shelves long before they appeared in the catalogue. We were always touched by the eagerness of our remote clients to get their orders in early.

Library orders came later, although some sent "holding orders" while they checked their own shelves. The rush usually lasted about four weeks and then tapered off gradually, although for six months or even a year after its appearance people would search the catalogue and hopefully send in orders.

We became rather famous for the careful way we wrapped our books. Newspaper and plenty of it, then corrugated paper and finally good quality wrapping paper and heavy gummed tape. This method did not always meet with approval, however. A letter appeared in one of our newspapers in which the writer voiced his complaint. "Why do most books we receive come wrapped up so fiercely that they might be intended for Outer Mongolia or even Inner Mongolia, although they only have to travel a few blocks?" The answer to this was, "Much better to have to use a little muscle in undoing parcels than to find bent corners on valuable or even inexpensive books." We used "book post" freely, only insuring when we sent very rare and utterly irreplaceable books or manuscripts. Of all the many thousands of books we sent this way very few were lost. One, I remember, was reported burned in a Colorado train wreck; the odd one did not arrive at its destination due to "enemy action" on the Atlantic, and one did not reach our client in New York during the terrific Christmas mail rush in the United States. This for twenty-six years is a remarkable record for our world postage system. Would that we could order the rest of our world affairs in such a systematic way.

Wartime regulations and restrictions came to our small office as they did to the large ones. The foreign Exchange Control Board ruled us and apparently our United States customers with a firm hand. The first time a notice appeared under this heading was in my catalogue Number Thirty-five, issued in 1944, although I think the restrictions must have begun earlier. This read, "Notice to United States customers—The regulations of the Foreign Exchange Control Board require payment in United States funds for exports to the United States." This appears in every catalogue until 1949. No hardship was entailed to us for the U.S. dollar was then worth $1.10, but it did lead to our daily struggle with "Form B.13." Every order of over $5 sent out of the country required five "B.13's" attached to it. These complicated forms were half a yard long and needed longer carbons to reach to the bottom, where I had five times to sign my name. Every book in the order had to be listed, the name of our bank given and the amount we expected to receive (and the date) in foreign exchange. These bulky sheets had to be attached to the outside of the parcels. We tied and gummed them on. At the post office they were removed and stamped. One came back to us—and how that file bulged with them; two went to our bank and the other two to Ottawa. When the cheque in payment arrived, we had to make out a yellow form and present it at the bank when we deposited the cheque. Now our bank was a domestic rather than a business one and the yellow forms distracted them. I think they were supposed to hunt up the white B.13 to match and send them on to Ottawa. One of the accountants begged me to dispense with these yellow forms. When I asked what became of all those B.13's they had of ours he, *sotto voce,* confessed that every six months they put them in the waste-paper basket. Whether this upset the arithmetic in Ottawa I never heard. It was somewhat of a relief when regulations changed once more and B.13's were required only for exports of over $25. The only compensation for us was the rather watered-down patriotic emotion we had of adding, however minutely, to the stack of foreign exchange for our country.

In the first few years, when I was struggling with the problem of pricing my books, I devised another filing system. After each catalogue was exhausted, I recorded on cards the price of each book, the date and number of the catalogue and whether sold or not. When the book was repeated the record, of course, went on the original card. Though useful in gauging the demand for each book it was a laborious piece of routine. I am surprised now that I was able to keep it up so long. I think I must have ceased to keep this record up to date with the arrival of the B.13 and the file then contained about three thousand cards. By the time my business changed hands the card prices were out of date, although as a bibliography of Canadiana they had some value. I gave them to the Toronto Reference Library as a slight return for the infinite variety of help I had received from that source.

I had a series of assistants during the years. They bore the brunt of coping with an owner who knew nothing of business routine and who could neither keep her accounts straight nor file with any certainty. Nevertheless, I had one asset which none of them developed and that was a prodigious memory. I particularly remember with gratitude Thelma Stevenson, Vera Martin, Katie Cassels, Sydney Grant, Elizabeth Stevens and finally Edith Baldwin and my daughter Glen.

My cat Madeline has appeared at intervals in these pages. While she could not, with any truth, be called an assistant she was assuredly part of the office personnel and did her bit in beguiling the customers. She was a small part-Persian lady with a winsome face and a tail that didn't come quite up to standard. She did not waste her charms upon us but should a stranger, especially a male, arrive, she was immediately in the foreground with all her wiles. She would climb to the top of the office ladder and sit demurely looking down on us, with her grey ruff circling her face and her slightly unsatisfactory tail wrapped round her front paws like the train of a duchess. If this manoeuvre failed to produce the desired response she would plant herself on the table beside her victim and slowly edge near enough to tap his hand gently. This usually produced a return pat and the remark, "Pretty cat you have." It was all she wanted and she allowed the sale to go through without further interruption. If she happened to be in another part of the house when anyone arrived in the office, her determination to get in by fair means or foul was comic. For twelve years she dominated the scene but when my ownership of the Book Room passed to other hands she lost interest in the clients and eventually in life itself.

In the twenty-six years of my Book Room career I issued forty-six catalogues and ten special lists. In these were listed 28,798 books and pamphlets. There were, of course, many repetitions but probably more than half were listed only once or twice.

To end this account of the inner workings of the Book Room I must attempt to answer the question I am often asked. How did you know what price to put on your books? It was necessary, in the first place, to learn the universal principle of supply and demand. To do this I studied the catalogues of reputable and well-established bookmen. I went to the Reference Library to look up auction reports but found them only occasionally helpful. I became familiar with the background of the books I had to catalogue from my bibliographies and histories. This took time but once learned stood me in good stead. The current values of the books, for instance, of Champlain, Charlevoix, Heriot and Weld, were not difficult to establish, but these were not everyday occurrences in the Book Room. The task became much more of a problem as the flood of later books increased and I was confronted with good books which apparently had never before been offered. It was necessary then, I found, to develop an acute sense of the value of the *content* of each book; this and the cultivation of a retentive memory for everything I had ever read or heard about a book was, I believe, the most useful faculty I acquired.

There is, of course, another factor not generally, I fear, taken seriously by the trade, summed up in the modern term "overhead." There is only one solution to this and that is to keep it so low that you are continually bumping your head and by doing most of the work yourself. So far I fear I have not thrown much light on the problem. Probably in the end we fall back on the ancient rule of trial and error. But looking back as a bookseller of long standing, I believe the crucial factor in successful pricing is to possess a deep and absorbing interest in one's vocation.

8. The Arctic in Books

To strive, to seek, to find and not to yield.

After I had bought, catalogued and sold books on the Canadian Arctic for a few years, I began to see a curious time pattern into which these books seemed to fall. For more than three centuries there appeared to have been high and low tides of public interest in these northern regions. This fluctuating demand for books on northern exploration aroused my curiosity but I never found any explanation of the reason for it.

One of my pleasant duties as a bookseller, to increase my knowledge of the Arctic, was to read from cover to cover the quarterly issues of *The Beaver,* the magazine put out by the Hudson's Bay Company in Winnipeg and edited for a long time by Mr. Clifford Wilson. This paper began in a modest way in 1920 as a monthly and at that time was little known by the general public. But in 1924 it became a quarterly and has gradually grown in public esteem till now it is considered the best two dollars' worth per year of reading in Canada and has stimulated interest in Northern Canada to an amazing degree. I had at one time a file of the early numbers which I hoarded with the hope of some day making it complete for I believed it would be valuable, but when I fulfilled this ambition and sold it, it was with regret I saw it bundled up and despatched to its new owner.

In 1949, while scanning the pages of the March number of *The Beaver,* deciding on which article I should read first, I noticed a heading which read thus:

> Explorations to the Canadian Arctic, an outline of sea voyages and land expeditions carried out by explorers of the Canadian Arctic from the earliest times to the year 1918, by P. J. Baird [then Director, Montreal Office, Canadian Arctic Institute of North America.]

Then followed an excellent bibliography of books on Arctic exploration, something I had often needed to check my own holdings on this subject. As this article extended into three issues of *The Beaver* and proved useful, I wrote to Mr. Clifford Wilson and asked him if it would be possible to reissue the three parts as one publication. I was delighted to hear he had arranged for this to be done and I forthwith ordered fifty copies. As it is now out of print, I think it might be interesting to quote extracts from Baird's headings and to tell some of my own experiences with Arctic books and explorers.

Baird's bibliography covers the great expanse of time and the many personalities involved from Frobisher in 1576 to Stefansson in 1916. Baird begins thus:

> The far northern reaches of Canada's territory are still among the least known regions of the Earth . . . As planes criss-cross the northern islands new straits and bays unsuspected one hundred years ago are being added to the map. Less than four hundred years ago this map started to take shape . . . It would seem worth while to list the major expeditions of discovery . . . a great mass of detail has been filled in by traders and travellers not mentioned in this brief survey.

Mr. Baird divides his survey into three parts. Part I covers the Elizabethan Age to 1800, Part II, the Golden Age, 1800-1860, and Part III from 1860 to 1914. Of Part I he writes:

> The first twenty-four expeditions constitute the initial period of exploration characterized by the vigour of the first fifty-five (Elizabethan) years, and much less vigour in the succeeding one hundred and eighty-five years. The Hudson's Bay Company was founded in 1670 and regular voyages (for furs) were made, but exploration languished till the brilliant northern sorties of Hearne and Mackenzie.

The earliest first editions of this period I remember to have had were Henry Ellis' *A Voyage to Hudson's Bay. By the Dobbs Galley and California in the years 1746 and 1747* (London, 1748), and Joseph Robson's *An Account of Six Years' Residence in Hudson's Bay from 1733 to 1736 and 1744 to 1747* (London, 1752, Charts and Maps). Earlier than this the books on exploration from 1576 are so scarce that only at long intervals do copies come into the market. Even the reprints of them by the Hakluyt Society are difficult to find.

Then, as Baird says, in 1795 came Samuel Hearne's *A Journey to the Prince of Wales Fort to the Northern Ocean. Undertaken by Order of the Hudson's Bay Company for the Discovery of Copper Mines, a North-West Passage, etc., in Years 1769 to 1772* (London, 1795). The book described his journey to the mouth of the Coppermine River, where traces of copper were found but, as will be seen, not followed up for over one hundred years. The English publishers were probably conscious of the new interest in Arctic travel for they brought the book out in the grand manner, in a quarto edition with four large plates and four folding maps. This first edition is now one of the classics of Arctic travel and commands a good price on the rare occasions when it comes into the market. The sale at the time it was published seems to have been a success, for the next year the enterprising Dublin publishers brought out a pirated edition in octavo with seven striking engravings and maps reproduced from the first edition. This was followed by a Paris edition in 1799 in one quarto volume and a two-volume one in duodecimo. I have had copies of all these early editions. Interest in Hearne's exploits may have been eclipsed by those of Alexander Mackenzie for it was not until 1911 that Hearne's Coppermine Journey was reprinted by the Champlain Society of Canada as their volume number 6. By a rare stroke of good fortune this edition was edited with an introduction by J. B. Tyrrell, the only man who had conducted an exploration over the same country since the time of Hearne.

Alexander Mackenzie's discovery of overland routes to the Frozen and Pacific Oceans aroused public interest to a pitch not reached since Elizabethan times. These successful expeditions took place in 1789 and 1793, but his great book was not published until 1801. It was given a splendid and lengthy title, *Voyages from Montreal on the River St. Lawrence, through the continent of North America to the Frozen and Pacific Oceans in the years 1789 and 1793* (London, 1801), and the publishers brought it out in a handsome quarto edition with plates and maps, although not quite so lavishly illustrated as Hearne's had been. This first edition, however, must have been a large one for although it remains one of the basic books for any Arctic collection, copies turn up with surprising regularity. The second English edition in octavo came out a year later and a New York one in duodecimo in 1803. Then once again a long wait before a limited edition was put out by Morang and Company of Toronto in two volumes in 1904. New York again followed suit and issued two volumes in the "American Explorers' Series." There was another Toronto edition known as the "Trailmakers of Canada" in 1911 and finally the Radisson Society of Toronto in 1927 reproduced the work in octavo with the title page and other features from the first edition. The map, unfortunately, in this edition is very poor and, as I considered it important, I had a photostat negative made from the first edition and always tipped in a positive of it when selling this otherwise satisfactory reprint.

Baird's *Part 2* begins:

> With the end of the Napoleonic Wars what might be called the Golden Age of exploration of our regions began, sparked by the British Admiralty, especially its secretary, Sir John Barrow. The period between 1800 and 1860 yielded a great deal of knowledge about the Canadian Arctic.

As this period includes the Franklin search, I have summarized Baird's pungent comments on it. He points out that John Rae at Lord Mayor's Bay was only two hundred miles from Franklin's then hale and hearty crew. They seem to have been a record-shy lot for had they built cairns on their landfalls they might have been rescued. Altogether the searching parties for Franklin included thirty-three ship-winterings, three summer seaborne voyages, four overland trips and two independent boat journeys. The greatest effort was in 1850-1851, but it remained for Rae in 1853-1854 and M'Clintock in 1857-1859 to bring back the only authentic traces of the lost party. The first edition of Captain F. L. M'Clintock's *Voyage of the Fox* came out in 1859 and ran into thousands of copies. The Toronto Public Library's *Bibliography of Canadiana* records their copy as the 12th thousand. I have had this book in many bindings and formats and probably for this reason it was never considered a rare book in my day.

There is one Arctic explorer of the early nineteenth century whose books never bring a high price although the reason is not apparent. Captain John Ross's first book, which came out in 1819 describing his search for the North-West passage, was an impressive volume with thirty-two plates and four maps, called *A Voyage of Discovery . . . for the Purpose of Exploring Baffin's Bay . . . and Inquiring into the Probability of a North-West Passage.* It was followed by Parry's *Journal of Discovery, etc., in 1821* and by Franklin's *Narrative of a Journey to the Shores of the Polar Sea* (London, 1923), both of which are now high-priced books. It is true that Ross failed in his objective (but so did all the others whose goal was to find a North-West passage), and turned back at Lancaster Sound mistaking a mirage or a bank of clouds for mountains, for which mistake he was not again employed by the Admiralty for ten years. However, in 1829 he was off to the Arctic again and once more produced a book. This he called *A Narrative of a Second Voyage in Search of a North-West Passage and a Residence in Arctic Regions during 1829 to 1833 and the Discovery of the North Magnetic Pole* (London, 1835). With the financial help of subscribers a splendid book was produced, with many coloured and black and white plates to illustrate the informal narrative. One of the plates I remember particularly depicted an Eskimo with a wooden leg from the knee. Ross relates that one of his shipmates carved the leg out of some wood they had on board, and devised a system of strapping, so that the one-legged Eskimo could wear it, and to make it a lasting memento, the name of the ship was burned into the wood. Little did I think that I would ever hear more about this episode. But I did.

In the early 1950's my daughter and I were asked by our friends, Mr. and Mrs. Lewis Duncan, to meet Mr. L. A. Learmonth, an authority on Arctic lore and travel. As an employee of the Hudson's Bay Company, Mr. Learmonth had spent his working years in the Arctic, his duties taking him up and down the coasts of the Gulf of Boothia and the surrounding waters and islands. With a taste for history he had studied all the great books on Arctic exploration and had arrived at some interesting and original conclusions based on his thorough knowledge of the territory. Mr. Learmonth was a good talker and on our part we were eager listeners. The subject of the fate of Franklin, of course, came up and this is what he told us. To the west of the Victoria Strait, where Franklin's crew are supposed to have abandoned their ship, with the body of the leader still in it, there are numerous low-lying and unexplored islands. There are two possibilities, Mr. Learmonth thinks; one, that Franklin may have been buried on one of these islands, or that the ship may have drifted west and broken up on reaching land. That there might still be some traces found is borne out by the discovery Mr. Learmonth made of a relic a year or two after we met him. In his archaeological research on the shores of Lancaster Sound he found the grave of Ross's peg-legged Eskimo—peg and all! In spite of this proof of the veracity of Ross, it is strange that his books bring only about half the price of those of his contemporaries.

Baird's *Part 3* is from 1859 to the beginning of the First World War.

This period saw the great days of whaling, supplemented by missions, trading companies and police posts . . . in that order. It witnessed the entry of nations other than Britain into the exploration field; the United States, Norway and the young nation Canada itself to prove her sovereignty and investigate the possibilities of development of the region . . . Since the First War too many parties have visited our regions for this catalogue to be continued . . . The Fifth Thule expedition led by R. Rasmussen 1921-24 was particularly important in its ethnographic results. T. H. Manning was the one responsible for the completion of the Foxe Basin Survey. Finally the voyage of the Royal Canadian Mounted Police schooner *St. Roth,* under command of Inspector H. A. Larsen completed the navigation of the North-West Passage in a single season from the Atlantic to the Pacific.

After studying Baird's article I began to see the truth of my theory that there were distinct breaks in the interest in Arctic exploration. The third period witnessed no exciting discoveries such as those of Hearne and Mackenzie in the first, nor the search for Franklin in the second, but it produced many absorbing books and outstanding explorers and was definitely more North American in character. It is about these years that I have some reminiscences to relate.

At the end of the third section of Baird's bibliography appears the first Arctic book I ever read from cover to cover. It is *Lands Forlorn,* by George M. Douglas, and was published in 1914. I was paying one of my frequent visits to Colonel Neilson's house in Quebec when I picked up this book, a presentation copy from the author, for the Neilsons and the Douglases had been friends for three generations.

The young author had been grubstaked by his wealthy and generous uncle, Dr. James Douglas, a Canadian by birth, with instructions to penetrate to the Coppermine River and to report on the deposits there observed by the early travellers since the time of Hearne. Douglas could not have chosen a more apt title for his book. He and his two companions were to make the arduous journey by boat to Fort Confidence, from thence to the Coppermine and to Dismal Lake by pack and to return by the Mackenzie river. It was a scientific expedition and every detail had to be planned and every contingency anticipated for they were to be cut off for nearly two years from contact with the outside world.

Most of the Arctic expeditions I had learned about at school or had heard of since had ended in near or complete disaster, or those who survived were so weakened by scurvy or starvation that their journeys made dismal tales. But this book was different. These men were good campers for they returned in excellent health, their scientific records intact and their task accomplished. According to Baird, this book ends an epoch in what might be called unaided Arctic travel. It was one of the first books I hoped to get when I was building up my Arctic shelf many years later in the Book Room. But it was long in coming into my hands and remains still a rare modern Arctic book. On re-reading it I confess I found it factual to a wearisome degree. Perhaps we had in the meantime grown accustomed to successful Arctic expeditions. It is strange now to recall how remote these places seemed; and yet in a comparatively few years I was dispatching my catalogues to a number of eager customers in Yellowknife, N.W.T. The I.Q. of the population of this place must be high, per capita, for orders came to me from doctors, male and female, from engineers, mineralogists, technicians and surveyors. The parcels of books had to be sent to Edmonton and from there via Canadian Pacific Airlines to Yellowknife. Intrigued to find themselves so near the pathway of early exploration, many of them asked for first editions of the books of Mackenzie, Rae, Franklin, Richardson and Back.

The next twenty years belonged to what might be called the Stefansson era, when through his many and well-read books he attempted to persuade the public that the Arctic is a friendly place, a term never before applied to these lands forlorn.

I had among my customers a goodly number of active explorers as well as many of the armchair variety. Most famous, in a world-wide sense, was Vilhjalmur Stefansson. Throughout my correspondence files are numerous letters in the fine, neat script of this Arctic adventurer and author. When he at last came to see me, I was at no loss to recognize him by his likeness to the more than life size bust in bronze, the splendid work of my friend, the late Emmanuel Hahn. This rugged bit of sculpture of Stefansson in his Arctic clothing now adorns the National Gallery in Ottawa. Stefansson sat for over an hour examining my stock while his taxi ticked away at my door, it being wartime and taxis, once secured, not lightly to be dismissed. It was stimulating to listen to this explorer, author and bibliophile discussing his two vast collections of Arctic books, one in New York and the other at his Vermont farm. I had in a small way helped to build them up. The New York collection he sold in the late 1940's to Dartmouth College, Hanover, New Hampshire, at a substantial price, and in 1957 the second collection fortunately came to Canada and is now in Calgary under the care of the Glenbow Foundation.

One small incident in this visit shows the generous nature of the man. It is sometimes a matter of boasting among collectors to "pick up a bargain in a bookshop." In this instance, however, Stefansson took the trouble to point out to me that I had priced very low in my last catalogue a book he knew to be extremely rare because he had never seen a copy although he knew of its existence. This was *The Cruise of the Florence* (Washington, 1879) by H. W. Howgate. A large expedition was planned to go to Cumberland Sound in 1877-1878, but only part of it was launched. A small bundle of those paper-covered books, as good as new, had been sent me by an agent in the Maritimes. Not finding any record of a price and having several copies, I priced them moderately, and the knowing ones got a bargain.

Captain D. C. MacMillan, too, had been a faithful customer although there were long gaps in his buying owing to his many voyages to the Arctic, I think twenty-seven or twenty-eight, surely a record . He was physically the exact opposite of Stefansson. His small, well-proportioned figure suggested a naval career rather than that of an adventurer. He, of course, combined the two professions. I remember him as a delightfully modest man considering his great achievements. Baird in his Arctic lists records his *Four Years in the White North* (New York, 1918).

Our own Professor J. Tuzo Wilson was another interesting client, especially during the years of the Second World War when he was on leave of absence from the Geophysics Department of the University of Toronto. Among other military duties, he was director of Operational Research at National Defence Headquarters and deputy director of Exercise Musk-ox. In 1948 Arctic travel had taken to wings and it was in that year that Professor Wilson flew over the North Pole. Both he and his mother, Mrs. J. C. Wilson of Ottawa, were ardent Arctic collectors.

In 1913 the Canadian Government seems to have awakened to the fact that the Canadian Arctic belonged to us and that we should know more about it. A large scientific expedition was launched known as the Canadian Arctic Expedition under the general direction of Stefansson. It lasted from 1913 to 1918 with, of course, some changes in the personnel, on account of the outbreak of the war in 1914. A tremendous number of reports was issued and these in the years to come caused many a headache in the Book Room when we were asked to produce copies of them. Dr. Diamond Jenness, an important member of the expedition, made a special study of the Copper Eskimo in the Western Arctic, their life, their folklore and their songs. Dr. Jenness wrote well, and the accounts of his studies would have been more widely read had they not been "Reports," for the general public seldom knows of their existence nor would they read them if they did know. Fortunately, Dr. Jenness seems to have realized this for in 1928 he wrote a book on his experiences and named it with a softly falling cadence *People of the Twilight.* As it was published in New York I fear the circulation in Canada was not as great as the book deserved. Personally, I enjoyed it as much as any Arctic book I have read and I was sorry that copies turned up so infrequently. Jenness lived for a whole year with an Eskimo family and became so fond of them and they of him that the final parting was something of a tragedy. Later Dr. Jenness' name appeared as the author of another book which in certain circles became a best seller. *The Indians of Canada,* first published in 1932 by the King's Printer, was the answer to the fervent wish of the booksellers of Canadiana.

There were other Canadian Government publications on Arctic explorations of which Lieutenant R. A. Gordon's in 1884-1886 is probably the earliest; but the one most in demand and, therefore, more eagerly sought by us, the dealers, is known among us simply as "the Ninth." If I should be asked by another dealer if I could use a "Ninth Report," I would reply, "Certainly, how much do you want for it," Officially this is the *Geographic Board, Ninth Report, 1910. Edited by James White. Place Names. Northern Canada.* The value of it lies in the list of personnel of all the known expeditions in Northern waters and the Hudson Bay from 1576-1910, and there is a large map in the pocket outlining the numerous routes. It was a happy thought on the part of someone, perhaps James White himself, to undertake this interesting project of research, and my customers all wanted copies to complete their Arctic collections.

Place names in the Arctic for the most part are duplications of those in the Old World; Churchill, York, Southampton, and so on. Could it have been a poet whose inspiration brought forth our latest appellation "Distant early warning?"

It is one of the characteristics of the book trade that we form an attachment for certain books. If it is a good book and copies turn up quite often, there is a certain satisfaction in being able to say, "Here is a book I can thoroughly recommend." In Arctic *desiderata* such a book was J. W. Tyrrell's *Across the Sub-Arctics of Canada, A Journey of 3,200 Miles by Canoe and Snowshoe through the Barren Lands*. The first edition came out in 1897 and was illustrated by Arthur Heming. I once had a copy signed by the author and the artist, with hand-coloured illustrations, but that copy was unique. A second edition came out in 1908. J. W. Tyrrell was the brother of J. B. Tyrrell who died recently well up in his nineties with a life behind him full of adventure and achievement in the more remote places of our country. In 1893 the two brothers made an expedition to Lake Athabaska through the barren lands to Chesterfield inlet. This arduous trip is the subject of the book. Later J. W. Tyrrell made many surveys and explorations from Labrador to Great Slave Lake.

The demand for Arctic travel books fell into the doldrums in the years before the Second World War and did not come out of this condition till near the close of the war. In this period, the first book describing the annual trip of the Royal Canadian Mounted Police to the Arctic was written by D. S. Robertson, a staff reporter of the *Evening Telegram*, who with two other members of the Press were invited to travel north on the *Beothic*. It is a book full of information not easily found elsewhere, but the publishers were loath to take risks at this time and only a thousand copies were printed. *To the Arctic with the Mounties* (Toronto, 1934) describes the voyage to the Arctic archipelago, Greenland, Hudson Bay and Ellesmere Island where the Mounties garrisoned Canada's farthest northern outpost.

During the last three years of the war the Book Room was frequently visited by men of the Armed Forces who had a taste for books and hours to put in while passing through Toronto. There were others whose duties were to take them into the sub-Arctic and who wished to know more about it. There was one occasion when I arrived in the office to find an enormous brigadier sauntering round the room inspecting the books with my cat Madeline comfortably seated on his shoulder.

In the late summer of 1943 a young man in Canadian naval uniform appeared at the Book Room door and asked in a very quiet voice if he could look at my Arctic books. He was fair and bearded and his light beige summer uniform with blue braid was strikingly becoming. I showed him my well-stocked shelves on this subject and without further conversation he went systematically to work. This, I knew, was the kind of man who wanted to be left to his own devices, and I too returned to my work at the table nearby.

After some time, still looking at the books, he remarked, "My wife has written a book on the Arctic, but we are not very pleased with it."

"Oh! But why not?" I replied, being rather surprised at so frank a statement. "Books on the Arctic by women are very rare." For so they were in those days.

"The trouble was," he remarked, "it was written during the early days of the war and the manuscript was sent to England for publication, and because of shipping difficulties we did not have the chance to correct the proofs."

"That was unfortunate, of course, but the publishers must have had confidence in the book or they never would have ventured to bring it out," I said.

"Yes," he admitted, "Hodder and Stoughton did very well. They sold the whole edition of three thousand five hundred copies in six months or so in England." And that is how I came to know about *Igloo for the Night,* by Mrs. Tom Manning.

Bit by bit I extracted the story from her reserved husband. How they had been married in 1938 in the *Nascopie* on its arrival at Cape Dorset in Baffinland, and a few days later had boarded their partly decked-in boat to begin their two-and-a-half-years' exploration journey up the coast of Baffinland, through the unmapped portion of Foxe Basin and finally down the west coast of Hudson's Bay to Churchill.

I wanted badly to read this book, but the Mannings themselves possessed only three or four copies, the not over-generous supply sent them by the publishers. Through restrictions of copyright none could be sent to Canada for sale. Tom Manning at the time I met him was on naval service, shuttling between Canada and the United States, advising on Arctic apparel and other matters, so I had to wait until Mrs. Manning sent me one of her precious copies.

I read the book with avidity. What manner of woman was this, I asked myself, who could write of such dangers, discomforts and weariness with uncomplaining candour; who could see the beauty in the lonely landscape and only momentarily recoil from the Arctic food which was to become her daily fare? As one reviewer put it. "(It) touches simple greatness as a book and as an adventure." I think, apart from having to wear Eskimo boots, my sympathy went out to her most when she complained of lack of fresh reading matter during the long dark days of winter. When I finally welcomed her into my office, I found her to be a delightfully feminine person, a Nova Scotian with a B.A. from Dalhousie, a true lover of animals, which made her as patient and full of consideration for my cat as she had been for their pack of sled dogs.

The Mannings had made some unsuccessful attempts to have *Igloo for the Night* published in Canada but had become discouraged. I felt I would like to try my hand at it. Here was a well-written Canadian Arctic book by a Canadian woman of which no copies were to be had in Canada. I knew that the *Canadian Historical Review,* each year printed a list of books on the Canadian Arctic and that if I could get *Igloo* into the right hands to appear in this periodical, it might lead to its publication. I asked permission to send my borrowed copy to the late Professor H. A. Innis, and to my satisfaction he reviewed it thus: "Among Arctic narratives the most important book which has appeared for some time is *Igloo for the Night,* by Mrs. Manning."

I do not claim the credit for the publication of the Canadian edition which came out in 1946, but I know my enthusiasm helped to get it launched. Unfortunately, the war restriction on paper and the not yet perfected "offset" method tended to make the book less attractive than the English edition. Nevertheless, I have no hesitation in affirming that no book published since, in my opinion, has told so ably the plain unvarnished truth about the Arctic. In the ten years since Mrs. Manning's book appeared, living conditions in the Arctic have radically changed. Never again will the Arctic traveller be so isolated, so exposed to the daily possibilities of disaster, and, as Mrs. Manning puts it, so occupied with the constant labour of merely existing. The book, therefore, in my estimation, ends another epoch in Arctic publications. There are many more books on these vast northern regions of ours that I would like to write about. It is a solemn thought that were it not for the printed word all the accomplishment, the effort and the sacrifice of the men of the Arctic would now be but so much water under the icebergs.

Even before Frobisher launched his first attack on the Arctic in 1579, it was Francis Bacon who made the discovery of the enduring power of books. In his *Advancement of Learning* he says:

> We see then how far the monuments of wit and learning are more durable than the monuments of power, or of the hands . . . (but) the images of men's wits and knowledges remain in books, exempt from wrong of time and capable of perpetual renovation. Neither are they fitly to be called images, because they generate still and cast their seeds into the minds of others provoking and causing infinite actions and opinions in succeeding generations.

It is a far cry from Francis Bacon of the sixteenth century discoursing on the power of books to Bishop Horden of the mid-nineteenth, labouriously working at his printing press at Moose Factory in the Canadian sub-Arctic. Beside me as I write, I see a sample of the output of this very press, and although I cannot read it, I treasure it for its imprint, "Moose, 1856." It was, of course, James Evans who, in 1840, devised the syllabic script in order that he might translate the Gospels into Cree and other Indian dialects while he was superintendent of the Methodist Missions at Norway House. It is recorded that he carved the symbols out of wood and with soot made his printing ink. A few years later John Horden of the Church Missionary Society (of England) at Moose Factory undertook to use Evans' script for his translations of hymns and prayers for the use of his Indian converts. These he sent home to England with instructions to have them printed and sent out to him for use in his Mission.

He waited long for the shipment and when at length it arrived he was surprised to find it contained, not the desired books, but a printing press and a font of syllabic type. The story goes that he retired to his own quarters for a week and emerged a master printer. Nearly one hundred years later I came into possession of a bundle of what we would now call "remainders" of the work of Horden's press. They are little octavo hymn sheets, printed in syllabic Cree characters on good rag paper and, as we say in the trade, "uncut and unopened." As James Bay, even the southern portion of it, lies within the sub-Arctic, Bishop Horden, as he afterwards became, may be considered the first Arctic printer.

There were, as I have shown, recessions in the demand for Arctic books, but basically this subject is one of the most important fields of collecting in our country. The great volumes now published annually by the Arctic Institute of North America are evidence of the vast amount of up-to-date information now offered on the subject.

To have had a share, however remote, in these Arctic adventures by merely handling many of the books was to me a great satisfaction. If I was still in business I would without question continue to keep up my supply of Arctic books.

9. What Subjects Interest Canadian Collectors or Book Buyers?

No hobby so old, so enduring, so respectable.

What books do Canadians collect? Before launching on this, one of my favourite subjects, I must try to clear up some misconceptions on this book-collecting game as it is played in Canada.

Do not expect from me advice on how to become a book-collector. The libraries are full of books on this very subject. I have dipped into many of them and remain convinced that you cannot make a true book-collector out of a person who has to be told how to go about it. In all my long years in the business no one has ever asked me, "How shall I begin to be a book-collector?" It is possible that this independent spirit is characteristic of the collector of Canadiana. I hope it is, and my experience points that way.

I cannot be quite so dogmatic on the next point. It has pitfalls and is not as simple to explain.

The term book-collecting is often considered synonymous with the acquisition of first editions. This is not necessarily so among Canadian collectors for several reasons. One of these may be that we in Canada are far removed from the great book centres where world-famous first editions repeatedly change hands at fabulous prices.

This lack of stimulation may have something to do with our indifference. Again, our own literary output as yet is known scarcely at all beyond our own borders and the books of many of our best writers have never gone beyond their first issues. Moreover, the collectors of these first and only editions are few, and these are, therefore, comparatively easy to acquire. This lack of competition gives little impetus to the first-edition quest. Fortunately for posterity, a few far-sighted Canadian collectors have over the years consistently gathered the first fruits of our writers and of these wise people I shall have some tales to tell elsewhere.

For the most part, however, the majority of Canadian book-collectors who came my way were more interested in the *subjects* they collected than in first editions in general. And they would probably have agreed with one delightful book-buyer who wrote thus on the subject: "Some of the greatest lovers of letters who ever lived—Dr. Johnson, for example, and Thomas De Quincy and Carlyle—have cared no more for first editions than I do for brussels sprouts." Augustine Birrell who penned this devastating indictment wrote many diverting essays on book buying and even on antiquarian booksellers. The small edition of his *Selected Essays* I have had since 1909; and in reading it again lately found it had an unsuspected Canadian interest. Birrell wrote in the preface: "When asked lately by my friend John Buchan to allow a selection (made by him) of my essays to be added to this series, I readily assented, for when all is said and done, circulation is an author's life." The book was published by Thomas Nelson, and probably cost me not more than a dollar. Buchan was then a partner of T. A. Nelson who had been his friend at Oxford. That the editor of essays became our most literary-minded Governor-General, and that the author has so much to say about secondhand booksellers doubly endears the book to me. I have read it many times these forty years.

Now, having made some statements that may be challenged, it is to be hoped I have left a loophole or two in case I have to withdraw in the face of an attack. I shall feel on firmer ground if I proceed to describe some of the many fields that have been successfully explored by Canadian collectors. I even may recall some ardent first edition collectors among them!

Canadian art as a collector's subject is a comparatively recent development. What makes it interesting is that it has an intense appeal especially to the younger generation.

It was William Colgate, an early researcher in this subject, who first drew my attention to the attractive vistas it opened. I soon began to tuck away odds and ends in any way connected with Canadian art in order to have something to show him the next time he dropped in for a talk. I had some early annual reports of the Ontario Society of Artists. The first of these were issued in 1873, when the exhibition was held at Notman & Fraser's Galleries on King Street East in Toronto. There were no illustrations but the names of the exhibitors were given and among them Verner's name appears so often in both the oils and water-colour sections that it is surprising why examples of his work are now hard to come by. Verner was born in Sheridan, Ontario, and was noted chiefly for his pictures of buffalo. It was not until 1886 that some paintings were reproduced in these little O.S.A. folders: they were the forerunners of many hundreds of pamphlets on the subject that passed through my hands. Mr. Colgate is the author of a number of biographies of the early artists, many of whom dwelt here briefly, leaving samples of their work, only to move on perhaps to greener fields. It was in 1944 that The Ryerson Press published

Mr. Colgate's fine book, *Canadian Art, Its Origin and Development.*

There are two approaches to Canadian art collecting. The purely artistic, "whose subtle power could stay yon cloud and fix it in that glorious shape," and the definitely historical side. Both have their devotees and are sometimes combined. My duties to all these collectors were to provide all the literature, old and new, that would enlarge their knowledge of the subject.

It is not possible here to tell of the many delightful avenues I explored with my customers. I content myself with stories of only a few of the collectors, writers and artists who came my way. The great collection of Canadian pictures, known as the William H. Coverdale Collection, gathered for the adornment of the walls of the Manoir Richelieu at Murray Bay, stimulated interest in the art of this country to a high degree. Old prints, engravings, maps, oil and water-colour pictures were gathered and catalogued under the direction of Percy F. Godenrath and by 1930, when the printed list appeared, they numbered 1,598. In the preface of this catalogue we read:

The deep current of Canadian history moving through three centuries has carried on its flood tide countless diaries, intimate letters, biographies, reminiscences and state documents which were the living chronicles of their time. But the ever-moving tide of generations has swept vast quantities of this rich substance down to oblivion. Diaries, unappreciated by contemporaries, are discarded and lost. Letters, often the richest of historical sources, are put aside and forgotten or crumble with brittle age. Even books, famous in their day, have been literally read out of existence. So, the passing of time has left only comparative fragments of the casual or deliberate writings of those who went before us in the making of Canada. Pictures, unlike the written word, seem to have survived the restless movements of generations.

I was told by Georges Ducharme that after the Coverdale agents had scoured the country there was not a picture of Canadian interest or even an illustrated book to be found. This dearth continued for a few years but in the mysterious way in which the secondhand market works it has since recovered. The Coverdale collection was a brilliant though somewhat wholesale effort, and the pity of it is so comparatively few people see it, and then only in summer months during which the hotel is open.

Marius Barbeau's name is inseparable from all that is indigenous in art in Canada and he continues to write with authority on many phases of the subject. His most sought after book is known as *Cornelius Krieghoff, Pioneer Painter in North America.* This was published in Toronto in 1934 by The Macmillan Company of Canada. Besides the life of the artist there is a chronological list of his dated pictures with notes and fifteen coloured plates. The painstaking work of the author is shown in the collected comments of those who actually remembered the artist. With all this research presented in one volume it is strange why the whole edition was not immediately sold out. It shows perhaps what difficult times the publishers were passing through as the depression deepened. I think the original price was about $7.50.

A year or so after *Krieghoff* appeared I was in Montreal and found copies of it on the bargain counter of a big departmental store for 98 cents. I bought about half a dozen. Ah, foolish one! A few months later I had a notice to say it was again for sale at the advanced price of $1.98. Once more I bought a few, but only a few. Then slowly the demand for it grew and has now reached such proportions that I dare not predict to what heights the price will go.

While Barbeau was preparing his list of Krieghoff's

pictures known to be in private hands, he visited me and inspected with much interest a small example of the artist's wonderfully detailed work in my private possession. Although it is listed in the books as mine, it was acquired many years ago by my husband, the late Dr. F. C. Hood. Barbeau says it is "a very early example . . . a fashionable cariole with lady and gentleman and a team of beautifully drawn horses on the St. Lawrence River, Mount Royal in the background, a French-Canadian wood sleigh and two men in white blanket coats on snow-shoes in the foreground." I have never seen another Krieghoff depicting this aspect of life in the province of Quebec.

An account of Canadian art as applied to books must include a reference to the work of C. W. Jefferys, not only as a painter and illustrator but as a historian in art and a most ardent collector of Canadiana. It was mere accident that the date of my retirement conflicted with the opportunity to acquire his amazing accumulation of books and pamphlets. Eventually this collection was bought and distributed by my successor.

The three books known as *The Picture Gallery of Canadian History,* The Ryerson Press, 1942-1950, covered the period from the Discovery to 1900, and stand as a monument to C. W. Jefferys' draftsmanship and his strong sense of Canadian history.

It was my privilege once to see one of the ways in which he acquired his exact knowledge of bygone days. A few of us, more or less historically-minded, travelled to Windsor, Ontario, to attend a meeting of the Ontario Historical Society. I think it was in 1938. After our Canadian sessions were over, we joined the Michigan State Historical Society in Detroit and were generously entertained by the Ford Motor Car Company at Dearborn Inn. Mr. Jefferys was in our group and being a fabulous raconteur entertained us vastly to the utter neglect of the delectable lunch our hosts had spread before us. Later we strolled across to the Henry Ford Museum which covers eight acres and houses in chronological order original examples of farm and household articles from pioneer times in America. It represents the emancipation of the agriculturalist and the housewife from a good deal of drudgery. This vast collection instantly fascinated Mr. Jefferys. Out came his sketch-book and pencil: his flow of conversation stopped like a turned-off tap. We became merely bothersome and restless men and women, and try as we would we could not induce him to come with us and see the rest of the model village. In truth, we never saw him again on the trip.

The most popular book among the rank and file of Canadian art book collectors is the two-volume set (sometimes bound in one volume) by Willis & Bartlett known as *Canadian Scenery.* The first edition appeared in London in 1842 and by some the one hundred and twenty-one engravings therein are considered better than those in the second edition. But any of the editions are desirable since they illustrate many remote and off-the-beaten-track places in Upper and Lower Canada, as well as several aspects of the well-known cities and towns. Bartlett, the artist, came four times to Canada between 1836 and 1852, besides travelling to many places in Europe and even to some parts of Asia, making sketches for engravings in illustrated books. He was an industrious young man even if he made little distinction in the aspect of the different countries he depicted. He died at the age of forty-five when on a sea voyage not far from Malta. Willis was the author of the extensive text, but I have never heard anyone refer to it, so overshadowed is it by the artist's work. The engravings are greatly improved by being skillfully coloured. Copies used to turn up quite often, but gradually the supply has diminished, though even after nearly one hundred and twenty years it has not reached the distinction yet of "very scarce."

It was in 1925 that Newton MacTavish brought out his handsome book, *The Fine Arts in Canada* (published by The Macmillan Company of Canada) with many beautifully coloured illustrations. This was followed in 1932 by Albert Robson's *Canadian Landscape Painters* (The Ryerson Press). The seventy-five coloured plates are not likely to be reproduced. Both these books went quickly out of print and have for some years been in the class of "scarce books."

In 1936 another spur was given to the study of Canadian art in the production of a number of beautifully produced small books on individual artists, with their biographies and examples of their work. The Ryerson Press was responsible for this inspiration known as the *Canadian Art Series.*

To refresh my mind on the development of interest in this subject, I looked through the volumes of my bound catalogues and found it was not until 1949 that "Art" appears as a separate section. It had gradually worked its way into the collectors' esteem so that it could no longer be classified with "Literature and Handicrafts." Art has in fact now become an important subject in any Canadian bookshop.

Mr. T. R. Lee, now of Montreal, was my most ardent Canadian art collector. He began this quest as a very young man and now still young is a great authority on the subject, and the owner of a unique library.

In my contacts with collectors of Canadian art, both in books and pictures, I was surprised to find how few knew of Dr. Sigmund Samuel's gift to his country, known as The Canadiana Gallery. Housed with so much dignity in Queen's Park, Toronto, this priceless storehouse of paintings, engravings, sketches and maps and even documents reveals our stirring history. Many of us have failed to realize how stirring it is until we see in this collection the many scenes of battle, murder and sudden death. While Dr. Samuel's collection depicts many other aspects of our past history, it is evident that our early conflicts appealed strongly to contemporary artists.

When I had to catalogue books on our early wars, I classified them as "History." Even the Rebellion of 1837-1838 appeared more appropriately under this heading. It was not until we were more firmly and widely known as Canadians that I used the term "Military Books" for accounts of our later wars and rebellions.

The Denison family was responsible for keeping alive the fitful military spirit in this country, occupied as it was chiefly with expansion and periodic "hard times." Colonel G. T. Denison's *History of Modern Cavalry* (London, 1878) was translated into a number of languages, and his *Soldiering in Canada* (Toronto, 1900) is considered a good account of the history of the North-West Rebellion. Every educated family in Ontario must have owned a copy of the latter book for it turned up with monotonous regularity for many years. The Fenian Raid of 1866 is documented in contemporary pamphlets by Denison, Somerville (a soldier and journalist) and a very few others who took part in it. These firsthand and very scarce accounts are eagerly picked up by collectors.

The two North-West Rebellions produced a rash of books setting forth the rights and wrongs of both sides and details of the military actions. My favourite publication on this subject is *Illustrated War News of the Rebellion,* issued in 1885 by the Grip Printing Press in Toronto, owned by the Bengough Brothers. There were eighteen numbers and the battle scenes of Indian and regimental warfare left nothing to be desired, nor did the text written by the war correspondents who must have been exceedingly new at the job of reporting military action. I had this interesting paper several times, but now it seems well-nigh impossible to find.

There was little sale for modern war books in the early nineteen-thirties. I found no demand for our brief records of the Canadians in the South African War, nor for the great volume of books, many of them heart-breaking, on the first Great War. I continued to collect them, although they lay undisturbed on their shelves, for I could not believe they were valueless. We were then, it will be remembered, discussing at length the futility of wars, and there was even no great stigma attached to young men who openly professed to be pacifists. Those who had lived their adult lives through the 1914-1918 strife refused to dwell on the horrors of that time, and I believe this had much to do with the lack of desire to collect military books. The Department of National Defence took twenty years to write the records and it was not until 1938 that the first two volumes appeared containing the narrative and maps from August, 1914, to September, 1915. As we were then on the eve of the Second World War the official record of the remaining years never appeared in print.

As the troubled thirties passed, the sale of war books gradually increased. This was not entirely due to the imminence of another war, but rather that a generation had grown up that knew little about 1914-1918, and was beginning to collect military records as historic documents. But with the approach of a new war, according to my files, by June, 1939, I was getting sheaves of orders from the Department of National Defence for books on the First Great War. Battalion histories were in demand and also such books as Sir Thomas White's *The Story of*

Canada's War Finance (1921). Then in November, 1939, came a frantic request from Ottawa for David Carnegie's *History of Munitions Supply in Canada, 1914-1918.* This was published in Toronto in 1924 by Longmans Green and my copy had long lain unclaimed. It was an important book and few copies came into the market.

Since that time there has been no lack of interest in modern war books, though a curious situation developed at the end of the 1939-1945 hostilities. Many of the troops remained in Holland for a year or more, and while there the literary and historically-minded commanding officers and others put their time to good account by writing regimental and squadron histories. These were printed in Holland, probably at little expense, while giving much needed employment to the Dutch printers and binders. The books were distributed to the troops and the more ardent brought them home as treasured possessions. Quite a number, however, must have turned theirs in for cash at the secondhand bookshops in Holland. When a few years later there was a demand in Canada for these books, our librarians began a desperate search to build up their collection of Second World War battalion histories. Even Her Majesty's Stationery Office in London sent me a long list of these volumes lacking in the War Office. In the meantime our Reference Library in Toronto, under the able guidance of Miss Lober, showed great resourcefulness in writing direct to the book-dealers in Holland and from them secured a fairly complete file.

There is now, I believe, a good deal of rivalry between the various institutions housing military books. The Canadian Military Institute in Toronto, through peace and war, has concentrated on enlarging the library and must now have exceedingly valuable records.

The library of the Royal Military College three times suffered loss by fire, but of late years has with marked vigour built up a valuable collection as well as an amply-stocked working library. It was interesting to me to help in this restoration for the College had played a prominent part in the youthful activities of our family circle. Life plays curious tricks if one lives long enough. When a few years ago I found myself in the precincts of the old "Stone Frigate" at the invitation of the librarian, I recalled vividly my first June Ball at the College when we followed tradition by dancing the last waltz by the light of the dawn. In those days my mind was not occupied with book titles and prices! Although it was now "fifty years on" I knew I was fortunate in having such a thoroughly congenial purpose in visiting the old landmarks.

Not far away I visited another military library to which I had sent books, housed in the old Tête du Pont barracks. The Defence College now occupies these historic quarters and it was encouraging to find that some archaeologically-minded group had excavated a few square yards of the compound to show a portion of the foundations of an early Fort Frontenac. The books in this library deal exclusively with the actual conduct of wars.

There is still another military collection to be found in the recessed walls of old Fort Henry. When orders for books came from this library I was interested to find that the bills were paid by the Ontario Department of Highways and not by the Dominion Government. As all good Canadians should know, the massive walls of the present Fort Henry never received a battle wound since it was built in 1832-1836. It was manned by British regiments for many years. Lately a large tablet has been erected in one of the rooms recording the names of these regiments under the true if infelicitous words (in Latin): "They also serve who only stand and wait." The curator asked me to be on the outlook for any shred of information on other regiments which may have been stationed here while serving in Canada. He is not at all sure that his record is complete.

The North-West Mounted Police, to give the famous force their original romantic name, was organized as a civil defence constabulary under semi-military discipline. The subject thus forms an appropriate link between military books and those on our Canadian West.

Many have taken up their pens to write, with more or less success, the tales and history of the Mounties, giving their books captivating names: *Riders of the Plain, Policing the Plains, The Silent Force,* and so on. There was always a steady demand for these books and many times they passed through my hands into libraries and private collections. When in due course I became the owner of a complete run of the annual reports of the Force from 1874 to 1911, I felt I had in all probability a unique possession. These firsthand accounts are without doubt the most interesting of all Canadian Government documents. From the time the isolated establishment of two hundred officers and men, with headquarters at Fort McLeod, had coped with the troubles between the Indians and the lawless elements among the settlers, had chased the whiskey pedlars over the border, and had taken part in the early stages of the Riel Rebellion of '85, they were seasoned police with a larger complement of men when difficulties arose during the Klondike Gold Rush of 1898. From then on the name has become as legendary as that of the Foreign Legion. I was determined that these annual Reports, an almost inexhaustible source of tales of high adventure and achievement, should not go beyond our borders, and when it was ordered by the librarian of one of our large military collections, I felt it was in a safe place—and might even some day be read.

These reports and a number of other documents on our

fisheries and border arbitrations, our conferences, agreements (and we appear to have had a few of these) and ponderous tomes on our Royal Commissions, came from the library of Sir Robert Borden, and was one of the last important collections I acquired. Mr. Henry Borden fell heir to all his uncle's books, but it was some years before he found time in a busy life to sort out what he needed; the balance, mostly official documents, he allowed me to purchase. When I examined these books I was confronted with the question: When does the information in a volume marked "Confidential" become public property? To press the point further, how can a printed book ever be strictly confidential, unless only one is printed, and that seems unlikely? Mr. Borden and I had to take chances on such volumes in this collection but felt no harm could be done provided they remained in Canada.

Books on the prairies strongly appealed to me. This attraction may have come from childhood memories of my father's protracted yearly trips to the Mid-west on business. At that time he manufactured binder twine and on these journeys he visited the centres, many of them remote from the railway where the newly-established farmers picked up their supplies. He had to take some ribbing from his friends when it was hinted that the grasshoppers had acquired a taste for his brand of twine. But these trips were dreaded by the family. The ever-present danger of prairie fires and the long delays in the arrival of letters weighed heavily on my mother, and although I was quite young at the time, I was conscious of her anxiety and of the general relief and happiness when the traveller returned.

It was not until 1950 that I took my first journey to the west with Butler's *Great Lone Land* as my travelling companion. As I neared Calgary and saw the Palliser Hotel rising on the prairie horizon, I thought it might be an interesting matter of statistics to find out how many people in each train east and west knew anything about the personality of the man after whom it was named. Palliser's *Report of 1863* is now the most sought-after document on this stretch of the prairies and the adjacent mountain region. Briefly the title is: *Exploration of British North America; Reports, Papers and Journals 1857-1859; Further Papers 1859-1860; More Journals 1857-1860.*

John Palliser was sent out to the west by the British Government to make this first scientific survey. With a large company of assistants he did a thorough piece of work, and although not all his conclusions were correct, his work has been used ever since as a basis on which to gauge the changing conditions of the region. British Government documents are not easily acquired in this country and for that reason alone it is strange that the Palliser Report has not been reprinted in some form during the past one hundred years. In the many books on the west I have examined, only a few mention his name and fewer still have quoted him although he was responsible for making the fact known to the British Government that the great American Desert did not extend many miles north of the forty-ninth parallel. His use of the significant term "Fertile Belt" caught and stirred the adventurous element in England and may have been responsible for the influx of settlers.

As Palliser was not far-sighted enough to foresee the possibility of a road to the coast through Canadian territory, it is somewhat of an anomaly that a towering hotel at the gateway to the mountains should bear his name.

The first time I was offered this famous *Report* I was fairly inexperienced, but had by chance picked up the information that it was a rare and important document. After I had bought it the vendor told me that several of the older booksellers had refused it. I had, however, no misgivings and was pleased with myself when I sold it at a very satisfactory price. Some years later I came across another book by John Palliser written before he began his scientific work in Canada, called *Solitary Rambles and Adventures of a Hunter in the Prairies* (London, 1853). I read this book with the hope of getting some insight into the character of the writer of the *Report.* I found him to be a fearless man though perhaps ill-prepared for his encounters with Indians and equally savage settlers and bears. The word "Rambles" seemed inadequate to describe his sanguinary progress through the wilds of Missouri. I thoroughly enjoyed this early "western."

Two men whose names are more familiar to Canadians than that of Palliser were sent on expeditions to the west by the Canadian Government during the same period. S. J. Dawson's *Report of Exploration of the Country of Lake Superior and the Red River Settlement and between there and the Assiniboine* (Toronto, 1859) and H. Y. Hind's *Report on Assiniboine and Saskatchewan Exploring Expedition* (Toronto, 1859) linked the east and the west as never before. These reports must have been widely studied for in no other way can I account for the steady stream of copies that flowed into my office nearly one hundred years after they were published. Dawson, the civil engineer, in 1868 opened up transportation to the Red River, the way later to be called the "Dawson Road" and over which he led the troops in the Rebellion of 1870. Hind, the geologist whose activities in public service were numerous, found time to write a two-volume *Narrative* of his western journey, illustrating it with his own coloured drawings. It was my good fortune to acquire a number of these original sketches and a colossal manuscript map of Lake Superior by the same able hand. These two men made explorations of the greatest value through some of the most difficult regions of our country, and while I do not grudge John Palliser his fine hotel, I look in vain for some public memorial to Hind and Dawson.

In contrast to these scientific journeys, full of vivid episodes as they were, there was another development in the west that ran almost concurrently. The very word "ranching" catches and holds our imagination and undoubtedly the most valuable and also the scarcest Canadian book on the subject is L. V. Kelly's *The Range Men, the Story of the Ranchers and Indians of Alberta* (William Briggs, Toronto, 1913). This is by far the most authentic book on cattle ranging and I was told by one of my western buyers that there is no other on either side of the border to compare with it. Although the book is not really old, nothing is known of the author. There is a rumour that the book was printed at the request of Kelly but that by the time it was ready (it is a volume of 468 pages and many illustrations but lacks an index), the author had disappeared. After waiting a suitable time the books were sold by the publisher at a substantial price and a good profit was realized. Nevertheless, it is strange how the history of a book can vanish. The booksellers always had long waiting lists for it.

Another authentic book on the same truly western subject was printed "for the author" by William Briggs, and appears in the collection of titles known as *The Ryerson Imprint*, compiled by W. Stewart Wallace. John R. Craig's *Ranching with Lords and Commons, or Twenty Years on the Range* came out in 1903. It is a spirited account of what might be described as absentee landlordism on the range. Craig was in charge of the famous Oxley Ranch in Alberta, owned by a London syndicate of which Lord Latham and A. Staveley Hill were the chief troublemakers, according to Craig. The book was so outspoken on the financial difficulties encountered by Craig that on its publication he was sued for libel. To conduct an enterprise in 1882 in the western prairies from London with no railway communication west of Winnipeg was to court disaster. It must have badly shaken the public's faith in "easy money" in Canada. I always found ready buyers for this on the few occasions when it turned up.

The name A. Staveley Hill reminds me of one of those curious coincidences which enlivened our days. Hill was the author of a book on the west from which Craig took generous slices, called *From Home to Home Autumn Wanderings in the North-West in Years 1881-2-3-4* (London, 1887). It is quite a pretentious book, although perhaps a little long-winded. One day I was seated at my table engaged in the congenial task of writing a catalogue, with piles of books on the floor all round my chair and the table well covered as usual with reference books and bibliographies, when the telephone rang and a voice asked for Staveley Hill's *From Home to Home.* I searched the appropriate shelves, but finding no copy had regretfully so to tell my would-be customer. I returned to my work and the very next book I picked up seemed to fairly shout at me, "Here I am," and sure enough, it was *From Home to Home.*

There are two misconceptions about how antiquarian booksellers make a living. The first is that they make enormous profits by selling only the rare and high-priced books. This is not possible in Canada, nor I believe elsewhere, for there are not enough Pallisers, Fleury Mesplets, Ponchots, Paul Kanes, and so on, to meet the demand. It is evident then that bookshops must stock the small fry of books, and to be quite frank, life would be dull indeed without these lively little bits and pieces. The second mistake, and this is common among those who want to sell us books, is that a bookseller has customers for *every* book. There are, of course, plenty of unsaleable books always in stock, but the curious catch is that you cannot be absolutely sure which ones they will turn out to be.

To illustrate this point I am reminded of a top shelf in the Book Room designated merely as "Canada." Here I stacked an assortment of small books written by hasty travellers to our west in the first ten to twelve years of the twentieth century. Bankers, mayors, businessmen and globe-trotters came in droves for a few weeks or months and returned to England to write about their travels. I classified them in my mind as unsaleable. However, once, to fill in a corner of the catalogue, I listed them at reasonable prices, even the one with the ridiculous title, *A Motor Scamper Across Canada.* To my surprise the western collectors snapped them up. It seemed in the past forty years these books had gradually become curiosities and most of them contained some picture in word or photograph that had disappeared from the western scene as completely as has the danger of prairie fires.

One more story before I have done with the west. It always enlivened my work when I suddenly discovered some present-day link with the past through a book I had perhaps handled many times. For instance, I had stocked and sold several editions of a book on western travel known as *North-West Passage by Land, a Narrative of an Expedition from the Atlantic to the Pacific.* The authors, so the title page said, were Viscount Milton and W. B. Cheadle. The first edition was published in 1865 and became famous because it was the narrative of the first *sporting* trip through the difficult Yellow Head Pass to the coast. The story was in reality written by Cheadle, the young and tiresome Viscount Milton being capable only of making trouble for his companions. The book had long been regarded as an old publication, the last edition appearing in 1875. To the surprise of the booksellers, *Cheadle* popped up again in 1931, this time as the author of the *Journal* of the same expedition. This was put out by the enterprising Graphic Publishers with two distinguished editors, Sir Arthur G. Doughty, then Dominion Archivist, and Gustave Lanctôt, a noted historian. It was revealed in the preface that the original Journal, now in the hands of a descendant of Cheadle, was much more detailed than the *Narrative* had been, and from then on there was a demand for the newer book. It was about 1951 that I began to get orders for all the copies of the *Journal* that I could lay my hands on from the offices of the Bechtel Company of San Francisco. This was highly satisfactory though puzzling. Not long after telephone orders came from the Canadian Bechtel Company. A long talk with one of the engineers of this company cleared away the mystery by revealing that the great pipe-line known as the Trans-Mountain was being built over the exact route taken by the two Englishmen eighty-five years ago, and the books were going into the hands of the historically-minded members of this company.

All the great books on exploration are basically works of transportation, but my collectors, while familiar with these narratives, were chiefly concerned with the gradual ways in which the problems had been solved. There are several books of fairly recent date devoted to this subject. For instance, Professor George Glazebrook in 1938 issued his monumental work called *A History of Transportation in Canada*. This is a useful history and contains a helpful bibliography; but the true collector enjoys gathering his own source material, in the form of maps, surveys, guide books and the early books and pamphlets on canal, lake and rail travel.

The words "carrying place" have a romantic sound to the ears of historically-minded Canadians, but few have so industriously searched for traces of these places with such scientific success as the late Dr. Percy J. Robinson, author of *Toronto during the French Régime—A History of the Toronto Region from Brûlé to Simcoe, 1615-1793* (The Ryerson Press, Toronto, 1933). Only five hundred copies of this book were printed. Dr. Robinson had not only examined maps and surveys but had himself tramped the country between the mouth of the Humber and the Holland Marsh and beyond. It was a thrilling experience, then, for me to be able to show him an atlas he had never before examined. Although issued without title page, this is known as Sir William Berry's *Atlas* and is considered the rarest English atlas. In my eighteenth catalogue (1937) I describe it thus: "A collection of maps published from 1680 to 1689, each double page having a handsomely engraved medallion with inscription. Only three other copies known to exist. This copy contains 30 of the 33 maps and includes the Map of North America, corrected from Sansom's early map." Dr. Robinson was much excited on examining the details of the Toronto area, as they confirmed his conclusions on the disputed route of the carrying place. This copy of Berry's *Atlas* is now in the library of the University of Toronto after having lain for an unknown number of years in an extremely old dwelling in Berthier-en-haut, a place on the shores of the St. Lawrence River founded in 1673.

Probably my chief connoisseur on the history of railway times was Mr. A. A. Merrilees. His business was a curious one: the collection and distribution of secondhand rolling stock. Sometimes when my supply of books seemed overwhelming, I would think of Mr. Merrilees and congratulate myself that at least my stock did not present the same storage problem as his, and yet he used to worry about the amount of space his transportation library occupied! Latterly it became difficult to offer him anything he did not possess.

Another of my "Transportation" customers was known privately among the staff as "our president". Mr. John W. Barrigar, who is the president of the Pittsburgh and Lake Erie Railroad, was always a welcome visitor. Full of knowledge on this vast subject he was willing to give my holdings his careful attention and for ten years ordered with flattering regularity from my catalogues. His large collection on railway transportation and allied subjects is considered one of the finest in private hands. It is fully indexed and now consulted by travellers and friends with similar taste who pass through Pittsburgh and call at his headquarters.

The Canadian Pacific Railway Publicity Department under Murray Gibbon had a good library on this subject to which I had the satisfaction of adding from time to time. The foundation of this library may be ascribed to Sir Sandford Fleming whose reports on the building of the C.P.R. are without doubt the most readable railway documents in Canada.

The late D. C. Coleman while Vice-President of the C.P.R. was a faithful orderer of transportation and other books from my catalogues. When a shipment of important books to him was apparently lost in transit, telephone and telegraph wires were kept busy in our efforts to find it. A few weeks later it was discovered to be still in the office of the Vice-President, while the owner himself had moved into the Presidential quarters.

Someone has aptly said that history is the first cousin to common gossip. One might go further and say that common gossip is local history and complete the circle by proving that local history is the very stuff of which history itself is made. Now my numerous customers for local histories must be described as book-buyers rather than book-collectors. They came literally from near and far and their keenness in the pursuit of the books they wanted was one of their most endearing characteristics. Sometimes they wanted books about the places they had always lived in, but more often they yearned to trace the history of the people and the institutions of their birthplaces, which knew them no more. I met many instances of the latter nostalgia. Once, for instance, a small book arrived at my office by a circuitous path. It was called *The History of Salmon Arm, B.C.* With difficulty I located the little town on the map on the western curve of Shuswap Lake; and because local histories are rare in that district, I listed the book in my catalogue. To my surprise I had a great many orders for it, not from the people now living there, but from those who had left to settle in distant places. Several times I had to write to the astonished and pleased author for more copies, and then in the course of a few months found myself only a few miles away from Salmon Arm on the shores of that lovely lake. I called on the author, a bookkeeper in a busy general store, and together we discussed the anomaly that only those who have forsaken the place they love display an active interest in its history.

An interlude. Shuswap Lake is kidney-shaped and this necessitates a long curving detour by the railway before it can pursue its journey in a westerly direction. The story goes that an engineer was asked to find out if it would be possible to span the lake with a bridge at Salmon Arm and thus shorten the route. When he arrived he took up a position on the rising ground outside the town overlooking the lake and there he sat pondering the problem for two years. At the end of that time he sent in a report that it could not be done; and so the train continues to take that picturesque and lengthy curve.

Fortunately, as in the case of my Salmon Arm historian, there are generally one or two in a community who have a strong enough sense of history to record the "common gossip" and thus build up a picture of the past.

While most Canadians are lamentably weak in the knowledge of the general history of their country, we have been treated better than we deserve by our historians. The Maritimes, Quebec and Ontario are quite rich in good county and provincial histories. There is a recent history of the Province of Quebec, by Robert Rumilly, which has now reached 29 volumes! Some of these county histories are well written and systematically arranged, though often they are merely a jumble of facts. It seems to matter little to the buyer if he really wants the information. Unfortunately, many of the small histories were printed locally and for a small public and are now extremely difficult to find.

Canadians, I believe, are not lacking in wit and humour, excepting in their books, and who should know this better than the present chronicler? It is refreshing then to single out one book that is rich both in humour and local history. *English Bloods,* by Roger Vardon, was another Canadian book put out in 1930 by the ill-fated Graphic Publishers of Ottawa and is now one of the most sought after of all the Graphic books. It tells the true story of a retired army officer who set up a profitable and entirely fraudulent business to teach farming in the backwoods of Muskoka to young Englishmen at £1,000 per annum. F. M. Dela Fosse, the author (Roger Vardon was a pseudonym) was one of the victims of Captain Martin; and he, therefore, wrote with authority. While the book is full of humour it paints a picture of the miserable and often desperate condition of the settlers through ignorance, poverty and lack of any of the amenities of life. There is, too, no better description of the beauties as well as of the sinister aspects of the Muskoka landscape. Mr. Dela Fosse lived through this experience and eventually settled in Peterborough where he became a successful librarian and died full of years and honours.

We in Toronto have been fortunate for we have inherited some priceless pioneer records in such books as Henry Scadding's *Toronto of Old.* There were two editions of this work, one published in 1872 and a second in 1878 which is considered more desirable in that there are several more illustrations and a map. I had a photostat of the map of Toronto made and slipped it into the first edition to make it more complete. How little would we now know of the original dwelling-places of the pioneer families were it not for this delightfully written book. One sentence I always particularly enjoyed. Writing of St. James' Cathedral, Henry Scadding says, "With our own eyes we saw [the pioneers] again and again engaged within these consecrated walls, in solemn acts which expressed, in spite of the vicissitudes which their destiny had brought with it, their unaffected faith in the unseen and their living hope in relation to futurity."

Many other books followed this one, general and particular, and culminated in the six volumes of *Landmarks of Toronto,* edited by J. Ross Robertson. These were published from 1894 to 1914, a veritable mine of information, sometimes unreliable, but what history is perfect after all? The story goes that the first volume was eagerly bought by the public and the editor quite naturally issued the second in a much larger edition only to discover that the buyers had cooled off and the sales lagged. When the third volume was ready only five hundred were printed. This revenge has plagued the booksellers ever since.

When I first appeared on the scene as a bookseller in Toronto, two of my earliest customers were the late Mr. T. A. Reed and Professor E. W. Banting, both keen searchers for news from anywhere about old Toronto. I was enjoined by both to be on the outlook for a picture of Moss Hall. I had, of course, never heard of this place, but was told it was a gloomy-looking structure built in 1850 in the University area on the rising ground now occupied by the Biological Building. In succession it had housed the Medical faculty, Art classes and in 1879 the Students Union and the first editorial quarters of the *Varsity*. It was called Moss Hall after the Hon. Thomas Moss, a B.A. of 1858 and eventually the Vice-Chancellor of the University. In 1885 it was demolished. The difficulty was, no sketch nor photograph of it had ever come to light, the only building in the precincts of the University with this distinction.

To me this was just one more incentive to make myself familiar with all the books, pamphlets and periodicals as they passed through my hands. But the prize in this instance was to go to Professor Banting. He was a fanatical if decidedly fickle collector and we never knew what his latest pursuit would be. One day he dashed into the office shouting, "I've found Moss Hall!" And so he had. In an auction room, he told us, he had bought a box of stereoscopic photographs and a viewer, the contrivance through which we as children became familiar with the Eiffel Tower and the Pyramids, and there, among the seven wonders of the world, he found a view of the University grounds, photographed by Notman and taken from the tower of University College. There in the southeast corner of the picture was the unprepossessing building called Moss Hall.

Mr. T. A. Reed was at the time preparing his history of the Athletic Association of the University to be called *The Blue and White* (Toronto, 1945). The photograph is reproduced and described in this book on pages 3 and 4.

It has forcibly struck me at times how dependent history is on the efforts of individual collectors. Mr. T. A. Reed's mass of information in books and pictures on the Toronto regions, its pioneer families, its growth and cultural developments, its churches and monuments, is the best example I know of this kind of collection. His pictures he turned into lantern slides so that others could enjoy them, and for years it needed only a small advertisement in the newspapers announcing a "talk by Mr. T. A. Reed on old Toronto" for a packed audience to turn up at church halls and school auditoriums. Mr. Reed was frequently consulted by authors who wished to have his opinion on the location in their books of historic spots. He told me that on one or two occasions his time spent in reading manuscripts had been wasted when the authors frankly ignored his corrections.

Newspaper editors know the news value of rare books and manuscripts. In most of the British weekly newspapers such as *The Times* and *The Observer* there is a small corner devoted to reports of sales at Christie's and Sotheby's. A battered cardboard box is up for sale, stuffed with a thousand letters in the fierce and elegant handwriting of Marie Corelli, so a reporter says, and he adds the comment, "Letter writing is a dying art. Never destroy an interesting letter." (*The Observer*, London, March 24, 1957).

It is questionable whether letters and manuscripts should be left in private hands if they are of historic or literary value. One member of a family may value and guard them while the next generation may cast them out. In my experience there are comparatively few collectors of manuscripts and letters in Canada. Those who have inherited such material have for the most part turned it over to the Dominion or Provincial Archives where it is catalogued and preserved. These institutions have made great strides in the past few years. The Ontario Department of Archives is now handsomely housed in a building of its own in Queen's Park after being moved four times in thirty years!

It always seems to me to be a cold-blooded act to turn family letters into cash. It is much better to do so, however, than to consign them to the dustbin. A taste for collecting does not necessarily run in families.

In my estimation the most ardent and discriminating collector of Canadian manuscript material is Dr. Lorne Pierce, who for many years has turned over his findings in this field to his *alma mater,* Queen's University, Kingston. In time to come it will be even more recognized as a valuable source of knowledge of our early writers. The collection began to take form in 1924 in the Douglas Library at Queen's University, and because of Dr. Pierce's friendship with our writers, such as Carman, Roberts, Campbell, Pickthall and many others, he gathered their literary remains, their first editions, and letters, manuscripts and other relics from their pens. He did not limit his collection to contemporary authors, but when opportunity arose went further back into the history of our country. One of his most prized manuscripts of the early period is Major John Richardson's *Desertion in Canada,* a work that never appeared in book form. Now John Richardson was one of our early and prolific authors and many of his books have a direct bearing on the history of our country. He was born in Queenston, Upper Canada, in 1796 and lived in Canada off and on till shortly before his death in New York in 1850. His two best known books are his *War of 1812* (Brockville, 1842) and his novel *Wacousta . . . A Tale of the Canadas* (3 vols., London, 1832), which has been reprinted a number of times up to 1930. But he wrote seventeen others, seven of them with Canadian backgrounds.

If I were attempting to give a definition of a book-collector in contrast to a book-buyer I would use Dr. Pierce's interest in Richardson's works as an example of the true collector's enjoyment in making his collection complete. To lack one of these important books would be a constant incentive to further search.

In 1946 Queen's University Library issued *A Catalogue of Canadian Manuscripts Collected by Lorne Pierce and Presented to Queen's University.* The collection has greatly increased since that date, one of the most interesting additions being the almost complete manuscript of William Kirby's *The Golden Dog* (New York and Montreal, 1877).

Books with "association" interest strongly appealed to me, although strangely enough I knew of no one who wanted them solely for their own sakes. Collectors were happy enough to possess one if they first needed the book itself to round out their collection. Those whose interest was in early printing in Canada were very glad to have a book or a pamphlet bearing the signature of John Neilson; and a signed Carman first edition pleased a collector of poetry. But on the whole there was no insistent demand for "association" books.

In my forty-second catalogue I recorded one which had both Canadian and United States interest. Where I acquired it I do not now remember, and it was not until I examined the book when preparing the catalogue that I discovered its unusual historic significance. It was Van Renselaer's *Narrative of the Affair at Queenstown in the War of 1812* (New York, 1836), which is considered a scarce book. While running my fingers through the leaves

I noticed it was vigorously annotated on the margins throughout. Then I turned to the title page and found that the author had presented this copy to General Roger Sheaffe, the date being Edinburgh, 1837. Now Van Renselaer and Sheaffe fought on opposite sides in the Battle of Queenston Heights and on the calamitous death of General Brock Sheaffe took over the command of the British and Canadian troops. To learn more about him, I looked in that invaluable source of information, *The Dictionary of Canadian Biography,* by W. Stewart Wallace (2 vols., 1945), and found that he had been born in Boston in colonial times. I may be stretching the point too far, but I like to think Van Renselaer and Sheaffe were friends when young. At least in happier times, the author of the *Affair at Queenstown* was on friendly enough terms to give his book to his old enemy, and Sheaffe evidently enjoyed adding in the margin his side of the story.

I have admitted elsewhere that booksellers often have unsaleable books on their shelves. The fault is not always the authors, but rather lack of learning on the part of the public. Among my unappreciated authors was a learned and witty Canadian who for many years graced the staff of the University of Toronto, Principal Maurice Hutton, Professor of Greek. I possess a copy of his *Greek Point of View* which has in my eyes charming association value. This copy belonged to Professor John Squair, long head of the French Department, who had pencilled annotations here and there throughout the text. In one he draws to the reader's attention that Hutton had credited Pope instead of Goldsmith with the well-known couplet:

"How small of all that human hearts endure
The part which laws and Kings can cause or cure"

How these clever men enjoy catching each other making mistakes, I thought. Then, as a matter of curiosity, I looked up the quotation in my old edition of Bartlett, and was amused to find it was neither Pope's nor Goldsmith's but Samuel Johnson's addition to Goldsmith's *Traveller*. If two learned men like Hutton and Squair, I thought, can muddle their Pope, Goldsmith and Johnson, the rest of us may be forgiven for our numerous lapses. On the fly-leaf of this copy is a tribute to Hutton's delightful style which I think is worth quoting. It is from a cutting taken from *Punch*, September 9, 1925.

Books about Greece—the Greece of yore—
  Are banned by some of our young lions,
Who, steeped in bio-chemic lore,
  Electrons, undramatic *Ions*,
Regard with an impatient deep disdain
All ancient knowledge, sacred or profane.

But here's a book that's fresh and new—
  Not like QUEEN ANNE, door-nails or mutton—
Entitled *The Greek Point of View*,
Writ by Professor MAURICE HUTTON . . .

So *Punch*, delighted here to find
  Judicious levity and learning,
Wit with high seriousness combined,
  Praise that is never undiscerning,
Although *Atlantic divisus ponto*,
Salutes Professor HUTTON of Toronto.

10. Some Postwar Acquisitions

Libraries are not made; they grow.

No Canadian bookseller can do without the many bulky volumes compiled with studious care by Henry James Morgan (1842-1915). His first biographical dictionary was issued in 1862 and called *Celebrated Canadians,* a Canadian history in itself, so detailed are the lives. This was brought up to date in 1898 and again in 1912. In between these dates his pen was not idle as any student of Canadian books knows well. It was in looking up the activities of Dr. James Henry Coyne of St. Thomas that I was struck by the intimate knowledge displayed by Morgan as a biographer. He begins his description of Dr. Coyne with the unusual term "Literary Investigator and Author." I had reason to know how apt this was when many years after 1912 I was called in to sort and eventually to buy the vast collection of books and papers that composed the Coyne library.

But before this happened Dr. Coyne's name and fame were made familiar to me by constantly handling and occasionally reading the volumes of the Ontario Historical Society. Many times he contributed to these *Papers and Records* and indeed he was responsible for one entire volume, No. 4, entitled *Dollier de Casson and de Bréhant de Galinée Exploration of the Great Lakes in 1669-1670.*

This is still in demand both by those who agreed with his conclusions and those who differed. One of his other contributions to the history of southern Ontario is his edition of the *Talbot Papers*.

Dr. Coyne's roots were very deep in Ontario soil for his grandfather had settled in the county of Elgin in 1817 where in 1849 James Henry was born. He was a brilliant scholar from his earliest years; one of those rare youths to whom examinations at school and university presented no difficulties whatever. Languages especially came to him without effort, and I was told by his daughter Margaret that he knew eight languages well enough to be able to act as volunteer interpreter in the police courts of St. Thomas when unfortunate foreigners came before the magistrates. He was called to the bar in 1870, and besides his law practice he, as a matter of course, became president of innumerable organizations in the county and elsewhere. In his day no man was better known in southern Ontario for his great ability and his fervent Canadianism. His biographer, unable to assess his powers in further detail, sums them up in these words, "An indefatigable historical miner and furrower."

When Dr. Coyne died in 1942, he left his library to his two daughters, but it was not until after the war that my correspondence with Miss Margaret Coyne began on the subject of his books. Many times a date was set for my visit to St. Thomas only to be postponed for reasons now forgotten. Every now and then I would wake in the night with the disturbing thought that someone else might be more persistent. At last in the winter of 1947 definite arrangements were made and I was off. Boarding the London and Port Stanley Railway reminded me of my efforts to find material for some of my "Transportation" customers. This railway was built by a group of Londoners who saw in it a more direct route to the United States via vessels across Lake Erie, and the possibility of making Port Stanley into an important centre of shipping. This was in 1856. The dream, however, was short lived and in 1875 the line was taken over by the Great Western and continued to run as an excursion route to the lake. My customers were interested in prospectuses and timetables of the early lines, and it was rather surprising how many I was able to produce from time to time.

Among the highlights I expected to find in the Coyne library was Thwaite's *Jesuit Relations and Allied Documents* (Cleveland, 1896-1901). There are seventy-four volumes in this splendid work, and as only seven hundred sets were issued and most of these are now reposing in institutional libraries, a set is considered a rare find for a dealer. It was a bitter disappointment on my arrival to discover that my friend Sol Wenroth had been enterprising enough to arrive unheralded a short time before and had very naturally persuaded Miss Coyne to let him buy the set. I blamed myself most of all for not being a little "quicker on the trigger." The rest of the books and papers had been shifted several times and confusion reigned, but as I had not had the chance to plough through such an interesting collection for a long time, I found I was thoroughly enjoying the work. It took me three days to sort and pack the collection, buoyed up from time to time by cups of tea and congenial chats with Miss Coyne.

After the transaction was over and I was ready for some relaxation in the open air, I asked Miss Coyne to take me to see Old St. Thomas Church, a landmark the inhabitants are so justly proud of. It was built in 1824, but the lovely rose-white brick a product, of course, of the countryside, has withstood the rigours of our climate all these years with little sign of wear. It is now perilously near the edge of the escarpment above the valley of

Kettle Creek; but even in winter the view from the surrounding graveyard has its beauties. No services are now held in the church, except on special occasions in the summer. May it long be preserved for its architectural and historical interest. One of the treasures of this church is the register, still extant, of the births, marriages and deaths of the first ten years of its existence. A transcript appears in the scarce Vol. 9 of the Ontario Historical Society Papers and Records, and thereby hangs a tale.

Quite a number of my customers were keen to trace their ancestors. It was difficult to devote much time during the day to help these seekers, but sometimes I relented in the evenings and allowed them to invade the office. Such a one was Miss Fraser. Her great-grandfather, she said, had five sons, all of whom settled in Upper Canada, and she was determined to trace the families of these men. She looked through innumerable book indices and quite happily annexed all the Frasers listed therein, even discovering family likenesses when we were lucky enough to find portraits. But I had grave doubts. At last I tried to pin her down to one Fraser who might have a name other than James or Andrew. "Well," she said, "there was one named Garrett and he lived in southern Ontario." A happy inspiration came to me; possibly he appeared in the copy of the St. Thomas parish register which appears in Volume 9 of the Ontario Historical Society Papers and Records as being born, married or buried. And sure enough there was Garrett's marriage to Lucinda House—January 5, 1824. My customer's joy on discovering this entry was quite touching. I decided, however, that things had gone far enough and closed the episode after selling her, rather reluctantly, the scarce Volume 9.

I was occupied most of the winter with the Coyne

books and papers. Manuscripts, handbills, pamphlets and transactions had to be sorted and arranged according to subject. Much of this thoroughly interesting miscellaneous material did not appear in my catalogues, but was disposed of for the most part in the office or by special lists to collectors whose tastes I knew. This is in many ways unfortunate as no record remains of this interesting material. But in my catalogue, Number 37 (1947-1948), several sections contain a great many of the outstanding Coyne books. The collection was especially rich in cartography, including the works by Gabriel Marcel, Gabriel Gravier, Sir Charles Lyell, and the monumental set of six volumes by Pierre Marcry entitled *Découvertes et Etablissements des Français dans l'Ouest et dans le Sud de l'Amérique Septentrionale 1614-1698, Mémoires et Documents inédits* (Paris, 1879-1888).

Never had I listed in one catalogue so many French editions of the important early travel books. Among them were Alexander Mackenzie's *Voyages, 1789-1793* (Paris edition, 1802) in three volumes; John Long's *Voyages and Travels* (Paris edition of 1794); Jonathan Carver's *Travels, 1766-1768* (Paris edition of 1784); and others originally issued in French such as Lahontan's *Nouveaux Voyages* (edition of 1728) and Lescarbot's *Histoire de la Nouvelle-France* in the handsome reprint by Tross of Paris, 1866. I am tempted to prolong the list, but I must content myself with mentioning Lafitau's *Moeurs des Sauvages Amériquains comparées aux moeurs des premiers temps* (Paris, 1724; 2 vols.) Many of the books had come from Parisian dealers, and carefully "tipped in" by Dr. Coyne were the original bills.

I think I may safely say such a collection will never come to light again in Ontario. I do not mean that there are not now more valuable libraries of high-priced books in Canada, but that this one combined an ardent collector's accumulation of volumes and papers covering nearly one hundred years of development in our country, including many of the great books produced in France and England.

In glancing through the four bound volumes of my fifty catalogues I find it significant that No. 37 containing the Coyne books was the second largest I ever issued, with 1,116 "items." No. 38 had 1,140, but the quality was not as high.

While every antiquarian book catalogue worthy of the name must be dotted with tempting highlights such as I found in Dr. Coyne's library, it was necessary for me to list also books recently out-of-print in demand by students, scholars, and librarians, and sometimes these were more difficult to find than an outsider would believe. It takes roughly ten years after publication for most books to begin to come into the secondhand market, and even after that time many of them may be found only in the working libraries of university professors, lawyers and other professional members of our society. Take, for example, two very different book: the first, W. P. M. Kennedy's *The Constitution of Canada 1534-1937* (London, 1938). This is the second edition but it contains the Statute of Westminster which brings it up to date and overshadows the first edition of 1927. The edition of 1938 went out of print almost immediately and after twenty years still comes very seldom into the market. The second book for which I had innumerable requests was G. F. G. Stanley's *Birth of Western Canada; a History of the Riel Rebellion* (Toronto, Longmans, 1936). This book was a casualty of the war. It was published in England and almost the entire stock was burned in the bombing of London. Why so few copies came to Canada is rather a mystery. Professor Stanley told me he had only one copy himself and was constantly asked where the book could be found.

I was fortunate therefore in the years when the world was slowly recovering after the Second World War to be able to buy several very desirable modern libraries.

Professor George M. Wrong I had known for many years. I had as a young woman attended, without benefit of matriculation, his lectures in history at the University. He was not in the strict sense of the word a book-collector, but in his professional life he had, of course, compiled a good working library and had a large miscellaneous collection of good books, purchased and inherited.

As we sat one day having tea together in his spacious and comfortable upstairs library in Walmer Road, he said to me, "My dear Mrs. Hood, my professional days are long over now and my eyes are beginning to fail. I want you to look over my Canadian history books and tell me if you would care to buy them. And in my basement are all the transactions and periodicals I have subscribed to for many years. I think you will find them in good order. Perhaps those, too, would interest you." I told him I knew I would be fortunate to get the books, even without looking at them, but arranged to inspect them carefully and to make him an offer. This I did a few days later and he agreed to let me have them at the figure I suggested.

When the time came to remove those well-kept books my heart was heavy for I knew they would leave a conspicuous gap on the library shelves. But on the day my assistant and I arrived, with an ardent admirer of hers to carry heavy cartons, we were saved the distressing operations of dismantling the shelves while the owner looked on, for on that day Professor Wrong was laid up with a bad cold.

In fairly quick succession I became the owner of two other professional libraries.

I do not think that Professor W. P. M. Kennedy had much sentiment about his books, he really had too many, for he talked cheerfully all the time my daughter and I were busy packing a large portion of his library. He had, of course, many books I needed badly, and I must admit they rather "went to my head," if such an expression is appropriate when applied to such ponderous volumes. In one corner of his library were several shelves devoted to books on the British Empire, as it was called from the last quarter of Queen Victoria's reign to the beginning of the Second World War. I think I was justified in believing that I might find customers for these, the best books on the government, economics, history and geography of the other parts of the Commonwealth. By way of an experiment, then, I bought these books as well as the Canadian ones. When I began to price them later for a catalogue I found the task extremely difficult as I knew nothing about their value, so to be on the safe side, I put them at temptingly low figures. The result was disastrous. Only a few were asked for, and I had to acknowledge that never had a section of my catalogue been so completely ignored.

The other professional library I bought at this time was that of Professor George Glazebrook whose reputation in the Department of History at the University of Toronto was an enviable one. We in Toronto considered ourselves fortunate to have kept him here so long. When the Department of External Affairs demanded his services in 1942, it was thought by his friends to be only a temporary absence "for the duration." He did return at the close of the war to his former university post, but not for long. His work in Ottawa had proved so essential that he was persuaded to return to it for good. I remember quite vividly the day he rang me up with the remark, "Would you like to come over and see my books? I find I am not to be a scholar any more!" I needed no urging and was well rewarded.

These three modern libraries were just what I needed to keep up my reputation as a source of scarce recent books as well as of the old and rare.

11. Publishers, the Booksellers and the Readers

In the old days booksellers were also publishers, frequently printers and sometimes paper makers.

"Publishers, on the whole, are shy beasts." So writes Lorne Pierce, of The Ryerson Press, in the first sentence of his revealing pamphlet, *On Publishers and Publishing* (Toronto, 1951). This declaration delighted me, for now it was evident that we suffered from the same malady and perhaps this accounted for our infrequent meetings.

Edward Weeks, a publisher of experience, addressed one of his books, *This Trade of Writing* (Boston, 1935). to authors and would-be authors, and a helpful book it is. Let us hope some publisher will in time address a book to the booksellers. It may even occur to some bookseller to write one to the publishers. But I hasten to say it will not be this chronicler.

I was, of course, definitely a borderline bookseller in that I confined myself to books bearing on Canada, and these for the most part non-fiction. As my agency business grew, my orders for new books mounted and my contacts with publishers increased though they never became close.

I have vivid recollections of my early timid encounters with the mysterious and aloof publishing world, housed as it seemed to me in large and impersonal buildings. My first approach was entirely by telephone. It took a great deal of courage to announce the name of my upstart business and any fortitude I possessed was usually shattered when an incredulous voice answered, "What? Spell it."

We Canadians are not noted, I fear, for our polite and leisurely ways over the telephone, and I confess I suffered much, at first partly because of my ignorance, from those whose business it should have been to give me accurate and helpful information. This situation changed greatly later on when it was possible for the publishers to put trained and informed men and women in this important post. After a time, when the Book Room became well known, a pleasant camaraderie developed between publishers' order departments and ourselves.

It may astonish the general book buyer to know how many publishers there are in Canada today. The latest list put out for the convenience of booksellers in a periodical called *Quill and Quire,* representing the book and stationery trade, gives the addresses and telephone numbers of no less than ninety-two firms. Of these twelve have their headquarters in the Province of Quebec, one in New Brunswick, and the remaining seventy-nine in Ontario. But more astonishing still, these ninety-two book distributing centres are agents for over five hundred firms outside of Canada. Do we deserve such a lavishly spread table of good fare?

Thirty years ago only a few publishers with little reward maintained their policy of bringing out Canadian books. Now all the important publishers' catalogues begin with a section headed Canadiana. The Ryerson Press has for some years devoted one complete catalogue twice a year to Canadian books. Writing as a bookseller I found this invaluable and consulted these catalogues frequently.

In my out-of-print work, I always considered worthy of preservation any early book catalogues of publishers, or those of libraries or private individuals. Comparatively few survived once they were superseded by new ones; but in the long run they are the best guide we now have to the reading trends of the period. I notice in one of my lists there is one of these catalogues printed in Boston in 1791, surely a long time for a small book catalogue to be tossing about this continent.

The most interesting catalogue in book form on the subject of Canadian publishing, which I have mentioned briefly elsewhere, deserves more comment here. The title reads, *The Ryerson Imprint, A Check-List of the Books and Pamphlets Published by The Ryerson Press since the Formation of the House in 1829, Compiled by W. Stewart Wallace, Librarian Emeritus, University of Toronto* (Toronto, 1954). The foreword, written by W. S. Wallace (my successor in the Book Room), makes excellent reading for the bookish person, and is followed by a list in chronological order, each year dated separately, of the names of all the books, with their authors, published from 1829 to 1954. A remarkable record which prompts us to think—perhaps we are not such an unread people as we have been led to believe. But even more remarkable, the compiler has been able to record the dates of birth and death, when it has occurred, of nearly all the authors. This book would have proved a valuable tool to me had I still been in business when it appeared.

The name The Ryerson Press was not adopted on the title pages until 1921. How well I knew some of its older ones, The Guardian Office, The Methodist Book Room, and Wm. Briggs. I could not mistake a Briggs book; it had a characteristic binding and was generally well printed. Looking over the list I see the names of many books that are still in demand could copies be found. It is tempting to name a number of them, but I must content myself with one issued in 1855 of definite Canadian interest and from the pen of a member of the remarkable

Ryerson Family. John Ryerson in his *Hudson's Bay: or a missionary tour in the territory of* . . . vividly describes his hazardous journey from Kingston to Fort Garry, and from thence to York Factory where he hears of the finding of the Franklin relics by John Rae. The book, with its eleven illustrations, is a credit to the publishers and well worth reading.

It was in 1923 that the Macmillan Company of Canada printed a most attractive small book, *A Canadian Publishing House* (Toronto). This well-designed and printed catalogue listed the names of the Canadian authors whose books the firm had published. The biographical and bibliographical notes added interest. As many of the books had gone out of print, it was not a commercial venture but rather a tribute to their Canadian authors. I treasured a copy of it for years.

Gradually, as I became better known I met the heads of some of the publishing houses, notably Lorne Pierce, Hugh Eayrs, Reginald Saunders, and after his service overseas, Hugh Kane. Most of the others still remained "shy beasts."

It was a red-letter day in my early career when Macmillans approached me to ask if I would undertake the first distribution of an important book they were bringing out. It was *The Journal of Duncan M'Gillivray of the North-West Company at Fort George on the Saskatchewan, 1794-95, with Introduction, Notes and Appendix* by Arthur S. Morton. (Macmillan Company of Canada, Toronto, 1929). This was the first printing of the *Journal,* and the edition consisted of only three hundred and fifty numbered copies. The book fitted into my work so well that I was only too happy to use my mailing list for sending out the impressive leaflet with my name on it prepared by the Company. The price was $7.50, and in spite of the unpropitious time it appeared I sold a great many copies.

Later I sold for Macmillan by special folder Lawrence Burpee's new edition of the *Search for the Western Sea,* though I do not think I had the exclusive sale of this book.

After these contacts I felt more at home in the company of publishers though I was rarely called on by their salesmen.

It was in 1935 when the Association of Canadian Bookmen was formed that the publishers came out of their cloisters and mingled with the common herd. The first president of this short-lived society was Pelham Edgar. It numbered among its members authors, librarians, critics, publishers and booksellers, and it was due to their combined efforts that the memorable Book Fairs of 1936 and 1937 were successfully organized and carried out.

I do not remember whether I was asked to set up an exhibit, but I know I was present only as an enthusiastic spectator. To refresh my memory about these two occasions I asked the Toronto Reference Library to let me see any material they had on the subject. To my surprise I was given a large scrapbook full of cuttings from contemporary newspapers and found it most entertaining reading.

The Book Fairs were held in the King Edward Hotel, the first one being opened by Sir William Mulock, and the second by the Lieutenant-Governor, Dr. Herbert Bruce. There were lavish exhibits of books by the fifteen publishing firms who sponsored the occasion, and whether it paid them or not, I remember the crowds, especially at the evening sessions, that gathered round the booths. There was an elaborate programme of lectures by eminent persons of the day (now, most of them merely names); there were plays, films, music and dinners, and at least one of the Fairs ended with a fancy-dress ball at which the dancers appeared as literary characters. Well-known authors appeared briefly and autographed their books;

among these were Arthur Stringer, Louis Blake Duff, Katherine Hale, Nellie McClung, Dan McCowan and Laura Salverson. But the biggest drawing card of the first Fair was Grey Owl. The reporters noted that more than two thousand people crowded the ball-room and watched this strange man in pseudo-Indian costume walk pigeon-toed in moccasins to the platform to make his speech. Then and for a number of years after there were many who believed implicitly in his Indian origin. There is no doubt his books had charm, and the demand for them has long outlived any sense of the fraud the author perpetrated on the public by posing as a full-blooded Indian.

Two exhibits of rare Canadiana at the Book Fair are noted by the newspapers, those of Lorne Pierce and the late A. H. O'Brien. Hugh Eayrs is quoted as declaring he had once purchased for $10.50 a fine copy of the first edition of Alexander Mackenzie's *Voyages . . . to the Frozen and Pacific Ocean, 1793* (a bargain indeed), and had a few years later refused $750 for it. My comment on this now is that it would have been more remarkable if he had actually received that amount for it.

The Book Fairs may have been an expensive experiment for the publishers and the Association of Canadian Bookmen, but the public thoroughly enjoyed the occasions. The ways of the world have changed greatly since 1937. The nearest approach to these elaborate affairs since that time has been the cocktail and coffee parties of individual publishers given generally to introduce one author and one book.

I have mentioned the Graphic Publishers of Ottawa several times in other places in referring to some of the books brought out by this short-lived firm. I have tried to trace accurate data from reliable sources on Philip Groves' connection with the Graphic Publishers, but I have been disappointed in my search. With a good deal of research I have compiled a list of the thirty-four definitely Canadian books Graphic issued between 1926 and its final disappearance in 1932. Of these only one could be classed as a reprint, namely, *Emily Montague.* Cheadle's *North West Passage* appeared as a journal, not a narrative as formerly, and Leacock's *Lahontan* has such an excellent introduction that it should be considered something more than a reprint. While the format and the printing of the books were not impressive, the effort was dedicated to Canadian authorship.

The printing firm of Rous & Mann of Toronto are not publishers in the strict sense of the word, but between 1925 and 1940 they produced three outstanding Canadian art books and a series of small books, all of them now prized possessions of the discriminating. These delightfully designed and executed books were not sold but given away to the fortunate friends of the company. The proprietors conceived the plan of seeking out small original manuscripts on Canadian subjects and engaging appropriate literary and historically-inclined persons to edit them. The limited number of copies issued and their importance as Canadiana has for years sent the antiquarian dealers scurrying round to find copies for their clients.

Publishing societies have never flourished for any length of time in Canada. The Radisson Society started bravely to reprint well known books but produced only five volumes. When I remember how often I have been asked for two of them—Paul Kane's *Wandering of an Artist in the Indian Country* and *Alexander Mackenzie's Voyages,* I fear we secondhand dealers are the only ones who made a profit.

The production and selling of books is probably one of the most difficult and hazardous forms of business men and women can attempt, yet from my own observation and experience it is one of the most satisfying.

It has been said that no great trade has a more obscure history than the book trade. Nobody has thought it worth while to make a record of his knowledge and so the records are irrevocably lost. Is it too late to begin?

I doubt whether it ever occurs to publishers or even to current booksellers to wonder what is likely to be the ultimate history of the gaily dust-wrapped books they publish, print, bind and display with so much pride and care.

We, the antiquarians, owe them a debt of gratitude extending back in time to 1440!

12. Finis—The Book Room Passes to Distinguished Hands

The constant turnover of old books is amazing. There seems no rest in this world even for folios and quartos.

My decision to retire came almost as swiftly and easily as had my determination to be a bookseller.

I was seated as usual at the large table in my office surrounded by piles of books and was about to take up my pencil to trace the words, "Catalogue 47" when suddenly the thought came, "You've done this long enough! Why not do something else in what remains of your life?"

The business was still flourishing, and until that moment I was conducting it with as much interest and vigour as I had from the beginning, but the incentive was now lacking. My two children were married, and I began to realize that I must seek companionship outside my house and work. I was anxious, too, to give more time to the work for the deaf. I had been partially deaf myself for many years and was intensely interested in what is now known as the Canadian Hearing Society, and had been a member of the board for some time. On my retirement I was able to act for three years as President of the Toronto Women's Auxiliary of this Society.

As I looked back over the years I knew how fortunate I had been. Although not endowed with unlimited strength, my health had been remarkably good. I had not made a fortune but I had been free from financial crises and had no bad debts, which speaks well for book buyers as a class. I had customers all over the free world who honoured me with their business and those whom I met in my office were highly intelligent and nearly all of them friendly. But like the "folios and quartos," there seemed no rest for the bookseller as long as his door remained open and his telephone connected.

All beginnings must have endings. But it seemed unthinkable and almost impossible simply to bring the business to an end. I began to look for a successor. Once again, with very little effort on my part, events were favourable, and I was able to pass the business on to the one person I knew who would more than do it justice. The name has been carried on and the quarters remain the same. An old customer returning would scarcely notice any change except that now a well-known and scholarly man sits at the office table. Dr. Stewart Wallace, on his retirement in 1954 after thirty years of distinguished work as Librarian of the University of Toronto, has become owner and proprietor of the Book Room.

People sometimes ask me if I miss my work.

"Not the work," I reply, "but my morning mail is not now as exhilarating as it was in the Book Room days."

Never again shall I feel as pleasant a glow of accomplishment as I did in bygone years on reading such letters as:

Dear Mrs. Hood:

Last night I spent a very pleasant hour perusing your fine catalogue. I have all your catalogues and treasure them as the most important series of Canadiana offerings that have been issued.

I would like to purchase any of the following that are still unsold . . .

Yours sincerely,

F. G. K.

INDEX